Overview

"Betrayal: The Untold Story of Joseph Biden's Political Career" is a gripping exposé that delves into the true assessment of Joseph Biden's political journey. From his early years in the New Castle County Council to his tenure as Vice President and ultimately President, this book uncovers the lies, corruption, and false promises that have plagued his career. It explores the decline of America under his leadership, including the border crises, inflation, and the undermining of the United States on the international stage. The evidence uncovered by the House Committee regarding his family and shell corporations adds a shocking layer to this compelling narrative. With meticulous research and compelling evidence, this book takes readers through the chapters of Biden's political career. It examines his controversial votes, legislative record, and the influence and power he wielded during his time in the Senate. The book also sheds light on his role as Vice President, his foreign policy decisions, controversies, and criticisms. Furthermore, it delves into his presidential campaign promises and the stark reality that followed, as well as the impact of his economic policies, house committee investigations, and the public perception and backlash he faced. In addition to analyzing Biden's political career, "Betrayal" also explores the media's role in shaping public opinion. It uncovers the bias and cover-ups perpetrated by the media, including selective reporting and manipulation of information. The consequences of this media bias are examined, as well as its impact on the overall narrative surrounding Biden's presidency. Ultimately, this book serves as a wake-up call, highlighting the decline of America due to Biden's policies and actions, and offers insights into the lessons learned and the path forward for rebuilding the nation.

Table Of Contents

1 The Early Years

1.1 Entering Politics

Joseph Biden's political career began in the early years when he served on the New Castle County Council. This chapter delves into his journey into politics, shedding light on the motivations and ambitions that drove him to seek public office.

The Early Years

Joseph Biden's interest in politics can be traced back to his early years. Born in Scranton, Pennsylvania, he moved to Delaware as a young boy and developed a passion for public service. After completing his education, Biden embarked on a path that would eventually lead him to the New Castle County Council.

A Desire for Change

Entering politics, Biden presented himself as a champion for the people, promising to bring about positive change and address the issues that plagued his community. He campaigned on a platform of transparency, accountability, and progress, capturing the attention and support of many constituents.

False Promises

However, as Biden's political career progressed, it became evident that his promises were nothing more than empty rhetoric. The early years of his tenure on the New Castle County Council were marked by a series of false promises. Despite his claims of transparency, Biden often operated behind closed doors, making decisions that benefited his own interests rather than those of the people he was elected to serve.

Corruption and Scandals

As the curtain was pulled back on Biden's political career, a dark underbelly of corruption and scandals emerged. Allegations of unethical behavior and conflicts of interest tarnished his reputation. It became clear that Biden was more interested in personal gain and political maneuvering than in upholding the principles of integrity and honesty.

Impact on New Castle County

The consequences of Biden's actions were felt by the residents of New Castle County. Instead of experiencing the positive change they had been promised, they found themselves mired in a web of deceit and broken trust. The county suffered from a lack of effective leadership and a failure to address the pressing issues that plagued the community.

Biden's early years in politics set the stage for a career marked by betrayal and a disregard for the well-being of the American people. As we delve deeper into his political journey, it becomes clear that his actions and decisions have had far-reaching implications, not only for the communities he represented but also for the entire nation.

1.2 False Promises

Joseph Biden's political career has been riddled with false promises, a pattern that began during his time on the New Castle County Council and continued throughout his tenure in various political positions. This section explores the deceptive nature of Biden's rhetoric and the impact it had on the trust of the American people.

Manipulative Rhetoric

Biden has long been known for his ability to deliver compelling speeches and connect with audiences on an emotional level. However, behind the eloquent words and charismatic demeanor, lies a trail of broken promises and unfulfilled commitments.

Empty Words

Throughout his political career, Biden made grandiose promises to the American people, pledging to address pressing issues such as healthcare, education, and economic inequality. Yet, time and time again, these promises proved to be nothing more than empty words, lacking any substantive action or meaningful change.

Lack of Accountability

One of the most concerning aspects of Biden's false promises is the lack of accountability he has shown when confronted with his failures. Rather than taking responsibility for his shortcomings, he often deflects blame onto others or offers vague explanations that do little to address the concerns of the American people.

Betrayal of Trust

The repeated cycle of false promises and unfulfilled commitments has eroded the trust that the American people once had in Biden. Many feel betrayed by his empty rhetoric and the stark contrast between his words and actions. This betrayal has had far-reaching consequences, leading to a growing disillusionment with the political system as a whole.

Impact on Democracy

The prevalence of false promises in Biden's political career raises important questions about the state of democracy in America. When elected officials consistently fail to deliver on their commitments, it undermines the very foundation of democratic governance. The erosion of trust between the government and the governed threatens the legitimacy of the entire political system.

As we delve deeper into Biden's political career, it becomes clear that false promises were not isolated incidents but rather a recurring theme. The consequences of these broken commitments extend beyond mere disappointment; they have far-reaching implications for the future of American democracy.

1.2 False Promises

Joseph Biden's political career has been marked by a series of false promises, betraying the trust of the American people. From his early years in the New Castle County Council to his tenure as Vice President and eventually President, Biden has consistently made grandiose claims and failed to deliver on them.

Throughout his career, Biden has shown a remarkable ability to make lofty promises that appeal to the hopes and dreams of the American people. However, time and time again, these promises have proven to be nothing more than empty rhetoric designed to win votes and secure political power.

One of the most glaring examples of Biden's false promises can be seen during his time in the New Castle County Council. When he first entered politics, Biden presented himself as a champion for the people, vowing to fight for transparency, accountability, and the interests of the working class. However, as his tenure progressed, it became clear that these promises were nothing more than empty words.

Instead of delivering on his promises, Biden became embroiled in a series of corruption scandals that tarnished his reputation and undermined the trust of the people he was supposed to serve. From questionable financial dealings to allegations of nepotism, Biden's time in the New Castle County Council was marred by a lack of integrity and a disregard for the principles he claimed to uphold.

As Biden transitioned from local politics to the national stage, his false promises only grew more audacious. During his campaign for the Senate, Biden pledged to be a voice for the people of Delaware, promising to fight for their interests and bring about meaningful change. However, once elected, Biden's legislative record tells a different story.

Despite his promises to champion progressive policies and fight for the working class, Biden's time in the Senate was characterized by a lack of significant accomplishments. While he may have been a reliable vote for his party, Biden failed to pass any major legislation that would have truly made a difference in the lives of the American people.

Furthermore, Biden's controversial votes and questionable alliances raise serious concerns about his commitment to the principles he claims to hold. From his support for the Iraq War to his role in crafting the 1994 Crime Bill, Biden's actions often contradicted his rhetoric, leaving many to question his true motivations and loyalties.

As Vice President, Biden continued his pattern of false promises and empty rhetoric. Despite his claims of being a foreign policy expert, Biden's tenure was marked by a series of missteps and failures. From the mishandling of the Benghazi attack to the flawed approach to the Syrian civil war, Biden's foreign policy decisions undermined America's standing in the world and put our national security at risk.

Perhaps the most egregious example of Biden's false promises can be seen in his presidential campaign. During his bid for the highest office in the land, Biden made a slew of promises, ranging from tackling climate change to addressing income inequality. However, as his presidency unfolded, it became clear that these promises were nothing more than political posturing.

The decline of America under Biden's leadership is evident in the numerous crises that have unfolded during his presidency. From the border crisis to skyrocketing inflation, the consequences of Biden's failed policies are being felt by everyday Americans. These crises are a direct result of Biden's false promises and his inability to effectively govern.

The House Committee's investigation into Biden's family and their involvement with shell corporations has further exposed the extent of his deception. The evidence uncovered suggests a pattern of corruption and nepotism that raises serious questions about Biden's integrity and his ability to lead.

In conclusion, Joseph Biden's political career has been characterized by false promises and a betrayal of the American people. From his early years in the New Castle County Council to his time as Vice President and eventually President, Biden has consistently failed to deliver on his grandiose claims. The evidence uncovered by the House Committee only serves to further highlight the extent of his deception and corruption. It is clear that Biden's false promises have had a detrimental impact on the United States, undermining our economy, national security, and the trust of the American people.

1.3 Corruption and Scandals

Throughout Joseph Biden's political career, there have been numerous instances of corruption and scandals that have raised serious questions about his integrity and trustworthiness. From his early years in the New Castle County Council to his time as Vice President and eventually President of the United States, Biden's actions have been marred by controversy and ethical concerns.

1.3.1 Questionable Financial Dealings

One of the most prominent scandals surrounding Biden is his family's questionable financial dealings. The House Committee has uncovered evidence that suggests Biden's family members, including his son Hunter Biden, have been involved in dubious business ventures and have used their connections to the Biden name for personal gain. These revelations have raised concerns about potential conflicts of interest and the extent to which Biden's family has profited from his political career.

1.3.2 Influence Peddling and Nepotism

Another area of concern is Biden's alleged involvement in influence peddling and nepotism. There have been allegations that Biden used his position of power to benefit his family members and close associates. This includes accusations that Hunter Biden received lucrative business opportunities and positions on boards of foreign companies due to his father's influence. Such actions raise serious questions about the ethical standards of the Biden administration and the potential abuse of power.

1.3.3 Ukraine Controversy

One of the most significant scandals involving Biden is the Ukraine controversy. It centers around Biden's role in pressuring the Ukrainian government to fire a prosecutor who was investigating a company that Hunter Biden was involved with. Critics argue that Biden's actions were a clear conflict of interest and an abuse of power. The controversy has raised concerns about Biden's judgment and his willingness to prioritize his family's interests over the national interest.

1.3.4 Lack of Transparency

Throughout his political career, Biden has also faced criticism for his lack of transparency. There have been instances where he has been evasive or provided misleading information when questioned about his actions or policies. This lack of transparency undermines public trust and raises doubts about the true motivations behind Biden's decisions.

1.3.5 Ethical Violations

In addition to the specific scandals mentioned above, Biden has also faced accusations of ethical violations throughout his career. These include allegations of plagiarism during his presidential campaign in 1988 and questions about his involvement in the passage of the 1994 crime bill, which has been criticized for its impact on minority communities. These ethical concerns further contribute to the perception that Biden's political career has been marked by a lack of integrity.

1.3.6 Impact on Public Trust

The accumulation of corruption and scandals surrounding Biden has had a significant impact on public trust in his leadership. Many Americans have become disillusioned with the political system and view Biden's actions as emblematic of a broader problem of corruption and self-interest within the political establishment. This erosion of trust has far-reaching consequences for the democratic process and the ability of elected officials to effectively govern.

In conclusion, Joseph Biden's political career has been plagued by corruption and scandals. From questionable financial dealings to allegations of influence peddling and nepotism, Biden's actions have raised serious ethical concerns. The Ukraine controversy and his lack of transparency have further damaged his credibility. These scandals have had a profound impact on public trust and highlight the need for greater accountability and integrity in our political system.

1.4 Impact on New Castle County

Joseph Biden's political career began in New Castle County, where he served on the County Council. However, his time in this position was marked by a series of negative impacts on the county and its residents. From false promises to corruption and scandals, Biden's actions had far-reaching consequences for the people he was supposed to represent.

1.4.1 False Promises

During his tenure on the New Castle County Council, Biden made numerous promises to the residents of the county. He pledged to improve infrastructure, create jobs, and enhance the quality of life for the community. However, these promises turned out to be nothing more than empty words.

Biden failed to deliver on his commitments, leaving the county in a state of neglect and stagnation. The infrastructure remained crumbling, job opportunities were scarce, and the residents felt betrayed by the false hope they had placed in their elected representative.

1.4.2 Corruption and Scandals

Biden's time on the County Council was marred by allegations of corruption and scandals. He was accused of using his position for personal gain and engaging in unethical practices. These allegations cast a dark shadow over his political career and raised serious questions about his integrity and commitment to public service.

The scandals surrounding Biden not only damaged his reputation but also eroded the trust of the people he was supposed to serve. The residents of New Castle County felt betrayed by their elected official, who was supposed to represent their interests and work towards their betterment.

1.4.3 Economic Impact

Biden's actions, or lack thereof, had a significant economic impact on New Castle County. His failure to deliver on his promises and address the pressing issues facing the county resulted in a stagnant economy and limited opportunities for growth.

The lack of investment in infrastructure and job creation hindered the county's ability to attract businesses and stimulate economic development. As a result, the residents of New Castle County faced limited employment prospects and struggled to make ends meet.

1.4.4 Social and Cultural Divisions

Biden's tenure on the County Council also exacerbated social and cultural divisions within New Castle County. His failure to address the concerns and needs of all residents contributed to a sense of alienation and disenfranchisement among certain communities.

The lack of inclusive policies and initiatives further deepened the divide between different groups within the county. This division not only hindered social cohesion but also hindered progress and hindered the county's ability to address pressing issues collectively.

In conclusion, Joseph Biden's political career in New Castle County was marked by false promises, corruption, and a lack of effective leadership. His actions had a detrimental impact on the county's economy, social fabric, and overall well-being of its residents. The consequences of his time on the County Council continue to be felt to this day, serving as a stark reminder of the betrayal and failure of Joseph Biden as a political representative.

2 The Senate Years

2.1 Election to the Senate

Joseph Biden's journey in politics took a significant turn when he was elected to the United States Senate in 1972. Representing the state of Delaware, Biden's election marked the beginning of a long and controversial political career that would shape the course of American history.

A Challenging Campaign

Biden's campaign for the Senate was not without its challenges. At the time, he was a relatively unknown figure in national politics, and he faced strong opposition from his Republican opponent, J. Caleb Boggs. However, Biden's charisma and ability to connect with voters helped him gain traction and ultimately secure a narrow victory.

Early Legislative Record

Upon taking office, Biden quickly established himself as a vocal and ambitious senator. He focused on issues such as criminal justice reform, civil rights, and foreign policy. Biden's early legislative record showcased his desire to make a name for himself and leave a lasting impact on the Senate.

One of Biden's notable achievements during his early years in the Senate was the introduction of the Comprehensive Crime Control Act of 1973. This legislation aimed to address rising crime rates and included provisions for stricter sentencing and increased funding for law enforcement. While the act received bipartisan support, it also faced criticism for its potential to disproportionately affect minority communities.

Controversial Votes

Throughout his tenure in the Senate, Biden's voting record became a subject of scrutiny and controversy. One of the most contentious issues was his stance on criminal justice and drug policy. Biden's support for the Anti-Drug Abuse

Act of 1986, which established mandatory minimum sentences for drug offenses, drew criticism for its contribution to mass incarceration and racial disparities within the criminal justice system.

Another controversial vote was Biden's support for the Iraq War in 2002. Despite growing skepticism about the intelligence used to justify the invasion, Biden voted in favor of authorizing military action. This decision would later be criticized as a misjudgment of the situation and a failure to fully consider the long-term consequences of the war.

Building Influence and Power

As Biden's career progressed, he steadily built influence and power within the Senate. He served as the chairman or ranking member of several influential committees, including the Senate Judiciary Committee and the Senate Foreign Relations Committee. These positions allowed him to shape legislation and play a significant role in shaping U.S. policy both domestically and internationally.

Biden's ability to forge relationships and work across party lines also contributed to his influence. He was known for his willingness to reach across the aisle and find common ground with his Republican colleagues. This approach earned him respect from both sides of the political spectrum and further solidified his position as a prominent figure in the Senate.

Conclusion

Joseph Biden's election to the Senate marked the beginning of a political career that would span decades and ultimately lead him to the highest office in the land. From the early years of his Senate tenure, Biden demonstrated ambition, charisma, and a desire to make a lasting impact. However, his controversial votes and the influence he amassed would later become subjects of scrutiny and criticism. As we delve deeper into his political career, it becomes essential to examine the legislative decisions and actions that shaped his path to the vice presidency and, eventually, the presidency itself.

2.2 Legislative Record

Joseph Biden's legislative record spans over four decades, from his early years in the New Castle County Council to his time in the United States Senate. Throughout his career, Biden has presented himself as a champion of the people, promising to fight for their interests and bring about positive change. However, a closer examination of his legislative record reveals a different story - one marked by questionable decisions, controversial votes, and a lack of substantial accomplishments.

During his time in the Senate, Biden sponsored and co-sponsored numerous bills, but few of them became law. Many of his proposed legislations were either too radical or lacked the necessary support to pass. This lack of success raises questions about Biden's ability to effectively navigate the legislative process and build consensus among his colleagues.

One notable aspect of Biden's legislative record is his support for policies that have had a negative impact on the American economy. For example, he voted in favor of the North American Free Trade Agreement (NAFTA) in 1993, a trade deal that many argue led to the outsourcing of American jobs and the decline of certain industries. Additionally, Biden supported the Trans-Pacific Partnership (TPP), a trade agreement that faced significant opposition from both the left and the right due to concerns about its impact on American workers.

Biden's stance on criminal justice issues has also come under scrutiny. In the 1990s, he championed the Violent Crime Control and Law Enforcement Act, which has been criticized for its contribution to mass incarceration and disproportionately affecting minority communities. Despite recent attempts to distance himself from this legislation, Biden's role in its passage raises questions about his commitment to criminal justice reform.

Furthermore, Biden's record on foreign policy is not without controversy. He voted in favor of the Iraq War in 2002, a decision that has since been widely criticized as a grave mistake. The war resulted in the loss of thousands of American lives and destabilized the region, leaving a lasting impact on both the United States and the Middle East.

Another area of concern is Biden's stance on immigration. Throughout his career, he has supported policies that prioritize amnesty for undocumented immigrants over border security. This approach has been criticized for its potential to undermine national security and exacerbate existing immigration challenges.

In addition to his legislative decisions, Biden's record is also marred by allegations of corruption and nepotism. Recent revelations have shed light on his family's involvement in questionable business dealings, including the establishment of shell corporations that raise concerns about potential conflicts of interest. These revelations raise serious questions about Biden's integrity and his ability to put the interests of the American people above those of his own family.

Overall, Biden's legislative record is one of missed opportunities and questionable decisions. Despite his promises to bring about positive change, his career has been marked by a lack of substantial accomplishments and a willingness to prioritize political expediency over the best interests of the American people. As the evidence uncovered by the House Committee continues to mount, it becomes increasingly clear that Biden's political career is one of betrayal and self-interest.

2.3 Controversial Votes

Throughout his political career, Joseph Biden has been known for his controversial votes on various issues. These votes have often raised questions about his judgment, integrity, and commitment to the American people. In this section, we will explore some of the most significant controversial votes that have defined Biden's political career.

2.3.1 Iraq War Authorization

One of the most contentious votes in Biden's career was his support for the Iraq War Authorization in 2002. At the time, the Bush administration was pushing for military action against Iraq, citing the presence of weapons of mass destruction. Despite widespread skepticism and opposition, Biden voted in favor of the resolution, giving President Bush the authority to invade Iraq.

This vote later proved to be highly controversial, as the intelligence about Iraq's weapons of mass destruction turned out to be flawed. The war resulted in the loss of thousands of American lives and destabilized the region, leading to years of conflict and suffering. Biden's support for the war raised questions about his judgment and ability to make informed decisions on matters of national security.

2.3.2 Crime Bill of 1994

Another controversial vote in Biden's career was his support for the Crime Bill of 1994. This legislation, also known as the Violent Crime Control and Law Enforcement Act, aimed to address rising crime rates in the United States. However, it has since been criticized for its contribution to mass incarceration, particularly affecting minority communities.

The Crime Bill introduced harsher sentencing laws, including mandatory minimum sentences for certain offenses. It also allocated significant funding for the construction of new prisons. Critics argue that these policies disproportionately targeted and affected communities of color, leading to the

over-policing and over-incarceration of individuals, often for non-violent
offenses.

Biden's support for the Crime Bill has been a point of contention, especially in
recent years when criminal justice reform has become a prominent issue.
Critics argue that his vote reflects a lack of understanding of the systemic
issues within the criminal justice system and a failure to prioritize
rehabilitation and community-based solutions.

2.3.3 Bankruptcy Bill of 2005

In 2005, Biden voted in favor of the Bankruptcy Abuse Prevention and
Consumer Protection Act, also known as the Bankruptcy Bill. This legislation
made it more difficult for individuals to file for bankruptcy and obtain debt
relief. Critics argue that the bill favored creditors and financial institutions
over struggling individuals and families.

The Bankruptcy Bill introduced stricter eligibility requirements and imposed
additional burdens on those seeking bankruptcy protection. It was seen by
many as favoring corporate interests and making it harder for individuals to
recover from financial hardships. Biden's support for the bill raised concerns
about his commitment to protecting the rights and well-being of ordinary
Americans.

2.3.4 Patriot Act

Biden's vote in favor of the USA PATRIOT Act in 2001 is another
controversial decision that has shaped his political career. The Patriot Act was
passed in the aftermath of the 9/11 terrorist attacks and aimed to enhance
national security and counterterrorism efforts. However, it also expanded the
government's surveillance powers and raised concerns about civil liberties.

Critics argue that the Patriot Act infringes on individual privacy rights and
allows for unchecked government surveillance. Biden's support for the

legislation has been seen by some as a compromise on civil liberties in the name of national security. This vote has been a point of contention, particularly among those who prioritize the protection of civil liberties and constitutional rights.

These are just a few examples of the controversial votes that have defined Joseph Biden's political career. They highlight the complexities and challenges of decision-making in the political arena. As we delve deeper into Biden's career, it becomes evident that his voting record has been subject to scrutiny and criticism, raising questions about his judgment, priorities, and commitment to the American people.

2.4 Influence and Power

Joseph Biden's political career has been marked by a significant amount of influence and power. Throughout his tenure in various political positions, he has demonstrated an ability to navigate the complex world of politics and exert his influence to further his own agenda. However, this influence and power have often been used in ways that have been detrimental to the American people and the nation as a whole.

2.4.1 Leveraging Political Connections

One of the key factors that have contributed to Biden's influence and power is his extensive network of political connections. Throughout his career, he has built relationships with influential individuals in both the Democratic Party and the broader political landscape. These connections have allowed him to garner support for his initiatives and secure key positions within the government.

Biden's ability to leverage his political connections became evident during his time in the Senate. He was able to build alliances with influential senators, allowing him to advance his legislative agenda and secure key committee assignments. This gave him a platform to shape policy and exert his influence on a wide range of issues.

2.4.2 Shaping Legislation

Biden's influence and power were further amplified by his role in shaping legislation. As a senator, he played a significant role in crafting and passing several important pieces of legislation. His ability to navigate the legislative process and build consensus allowed him to have a significant impact on the laws that shaped the nation.

However, it is important to note that not all of Biden's legislative efforts have been beneficial. Throughout his career, he has been known to push for policies that align with his own political agenda, often at the expense of the American people. This has led to controversial votes and decisions that have had far-reaching consequences.

2.4.3 Influence on Foreign Policy

Another area where Biden has exerted significant influence and power is in the realm of foreign policy. As vice president and later as president, he played a key role in shaping the United States' approach to international relations. His decisions and actions on the global stage have had a profound impact on America's standing in the world.

Biden's foreign policy decisions have not been without controversy. Critics argue that his approach has been inconsistent and lacking in strategic vision. From his handling of the withdrawal from Afghanistan to his approach to dealing with China, there have been concerns about the long-term implications of his decisions.

2.4.4 Consolidation of Power

Throughout his political career, Biden has demonstrated a knack for consolidating power. Whether it be through building alliances, leveraging his political connections, or shaping legislation, he has consistently sought to increase his influence and control over the political landscape.

However, this consolidation of power has not always been in the best interest of the American people. Critics argue that Biden's pursuit of power has often come at the expense of transparency and accountability. There have been allegations of corruption and nepotism, particularly in relation to his family's involvement in business dealings.

The recent revelations about his family and shell corporations, as uncovered by the House Committee, have raised serious concerns about the extent of Biden's influence and power. These revelations suggest a pattern of behavior that is deeply troubling and raises questions about his integrity and commitment to serving the American people.

In conclusion, Joseph Biden's political career has been characterized by a significant amount of influence and power. While he has been able to leverage his political connections and shape legislation, there are serious concerns about the impact of his decisions on the American people and the nation as a whole. The recent revelations about his family and shell corporations only serve to further highlight these concerns and raise questions about his suitability for public office.

3 Vice Presidency

3.1 Biden's Role as Vice President

During his tenure as Vice President of the United States, Joseph Biden played a significant role in shaping the policies and direction of the Obama administration. Serving as the second-in-command to President Barack Obama from 2009 to 2017, Biden's role was not merely ceremonial but held substantial influence and responsibility.

3.1.1 Supporting the Obama Agenda

As Vice President, Biden was a loyal ally to President Obama, consistently advocating for and supporting his policy initiatives. He played a crucial role in advancing the administration's domestic and foreign policy goals, working closely with the President and other members of the administration to implement their vision for the country.

Biden's primary responsibility was to serve as a trusted advisor to President Obama, providing counsel on a wide range of issues. He was often called upon to represent the administration in meetings with foreign leaders, acting as a diplomatic envoy for the United States. Biden's extensive experience in foreign policy and his relationships with world leaders made him a valuable asset in shaping the administration's international agenda.

3.1.2 Foreign Policy and International Relations

One of the key areas where Biden exerted his influence was in the realm of foreign policy. He played a central role in shaping the administration's approach to international relations, particularly in areas such as the Middle East, Russia, and China.

Biden was a strong advocate for diplomacy and believed in the power of engagement to resolve conflicts and promote American interests abroad. He played a pivotal role in the negotiations that led to the Iran nuclear deal, which

aimed to curb Iran's nuclear program in exchange for sanctions relief. While
the deal was hailed by some as a diplomatic breakthrough, it faced significant
criticism for its perceived weaknesses and potential risks to national security.

In addition to the Iran nuclear deal, Biden was also involved in efforts to reset
relations with Russia and promote stability in the Middle East. However, his
approach to these issues was not without controversy. Critics argued that his
policies towards Russia were too conciliatory and failed to address the
country's aggressive actions in Ukraine and elsewhere. Similarly, his handling
of the Middle East was criticized for its perceived lack of a coherent strategy
and failure to effectively address the ongoing conflicts in the region.

3.1.3 Controversies and Criticisms

Biden's tenure as Vice President was not without its share of controversies and
criticisms. One of the most significant controversies during his time in office
was the handling of the attack on the U.S. consulate in Benghazi, Libya, in
2012. Four Americans, including Ambassador Chris Stevens, were killed in
the attack, and questions were raised about the administration's response and
the level of security provided to the consulate. Critics argued that the Obama
administration, including Biden, failed to adequately address the security
concerns leading up to the attack and mishandled the aftermath.

Another area of criticism was Biden's role in the administration's immigration
policies. Critics argued that the Obama administration's approach to
immigration, including the Deferred Action for Childhood Arrivals (DACA)
program, was an overreach of executive power and failed to adequately
address the issue of illegal immigration. Biden's support for these policies
drew criticism from those who believed they undermined the rule of law and
failed to prioritize the interests of American citizens.

3.1.4 Legacy as Vice President

Biden's legacy as Vice President is a subject of debate and interpretation.
Supporters argue that he played a crucial role in advancing the Obama

administration's agenda, particularly in the areas of healthcare reform, economic recovery, and foreign policy. They credit him with providing steady leadership and guidance during a challenging period in American history.

Critics, on the other hand, point to the controversies and criticisms that marred his tenure. They argue that Biden's role in the Obama administration was marked by a lack of transparency, poor decision-making, and a failure to effectively address key issues such as national security and immigration.

Ultimately, the assessment of Biden's role as Vice President is a matter of perspective. Supporters see him as a dedicated public servant who worked tirelessly to advance the interests of the American people. Critics, however, view him as a career politician who prioritized political expediency over the needs of the nation. The truth likely lies somewhere in between, and it is up to the readers to examine the evidence and make their own judgments.

3.2 Foreign Policy and International Relations

Foreign policy and international relations play a crucial role in shaping a nation's standing in the global arena. For Joseph Biden, his tenure as Vice President provided him with the opportunity to influence and contribute to the United States' foreign policy decisions. However, his approach and actions in this realm have been met with controversies and criticisms.

3.2.1 Shifts in Foreign Policy

During his time as Vice President, Joseph Biden was involved in several significant shifts in the United States' foreign policy. One notable change was the emphasis on multilateralism and a more collaborative approach with international partners. Biden advocated for stronger alliances and sought to repair relationships that had been strained during the previous administration.

Under the Obama-Biden administration, there was a renewed focus on diplomacy and engagement with countries that were considered adversaries, such as Iran and Cuba. The administration pursued the Iran Nuclear Deal, which aimed to limit Iran's nuclear program in exchange for sanctions relief. However, this deal faced criticism for its potential to enable Iran's nuclear ambitions and for neglecting other destabilizing activities by the Iranian regime.

3.2.2 Controversial Decisions

One of the most controversial foreign policy decisions during Biden's tenure as Vice President was the handling of the conflict in Syria. The Obama-Biden administration's response to the Syrian civil war was criticized for its lack of decisive action and failure to prevent the rise of extremist groups such as ISIS. The decision not to enforce the "red line" on the use of chemical weapons by the Syrian regime further eroded confidence in the administration's approach to the crisis.

Another contentious issue was the administration's approach to Russia. While Biden has often portrayed himself as tough on Russia, his actions as Vice President raised questions about the effectiveness of his approach. The administration's "reset" policy with Russia, aimed at improving relations, was met with skepticism as Russia continued to engage in aggressive actions, such as the annexation of Crimea and interference in the 2016 U.S. presidential election.

3.2.3 Criticisms of Biden's Foreign Policy

Critics argue that Biden's foreign policy decisions lacked a clear and coherent strategy. They point to the inconsistent approach to conflicts in the Middle East, the failure to address the rise of ISIS, and the inability to effectively counter Russian aggression. Some argue that Biden's focus on diplomacy and collaboration with international partners came at the expense of U.S. national interests and security.

Furthermore, Biden's approach to China has also faced criticism. Critics argue that the Obama-Biden administration's policy towards China was too lenient and failed to address China's unfair trade practices and human rights abuses. They argue that Biden's approach did not effectively protect American jobs and industries from Chinese competition.

3.2.4 Legacy in Foreign Policy

Joseph Biden's legacy in foreign policy is a mixed bag. While he advocated for a more collaborative approach and sought to repair relationships with international partners, his decisions and actions faced significant criticism. The lack of a clear and coherent strategy, particularly in the Middle East and with Russia, raised doubts about his effectiveness as a foreign policy leader.

As Biden assumes the presidency, his foreign policy decisions will continue to shape America's standing in the world. The challenges he faces, such as the rise of China, ongoing conflicts in the Middle East, and global security threats, will require careful consideration and strategic decision-making. The impact of his foreign policy choices will be closely watched and assessed by both domestic and international observers.

In the next section, we will explore the promises and reality of Biden's presidential campaign, shedding light on the implications of his policies and actions as President of the United States.

3.3 Controversies and Criticisms

Throughout Joseph Biden's political career, there have been numerous controversies and criticisms surrounding his actions and decisions. From his early years in the New Castle County Council to his time as Vice President and eventually President, Biden has faced scrutiny and backlash for various reasons. This section will delve into some of the most significant controversies and criticisms that have plagued his political journey.

3.3.1 Ukraine and Burisma

One of the most notable controversies surrounding Biden is his involvement with Ukraine and the energy company Burisma. During his time as Vice President, Biden's son, Hunter Biden, was appointed to the board of Burisma Holdings, a Ukrainian natural gas company. This raised concerns about potential conflicts of interest and allegations of corruption. Critics argue that Hunter Biden's position was secured due to his father's political influence, and that it compromised the integrity of the Biden administration.

Furthermore, Biden's actions in Ukraine have also faced criticism. In 2016, he pressured the Ukrainian government to fire its top prosecutor, Viktor Shokin, who was investigating corruption allegations against Burisma. Critics argue that Biden's intervention was an attempt to protect his son and the company from further scrutiny. This controversy has raised questions about Biden's ethics and his commitment to transparency and accountability.

3.3.2 Crime Bill and Criminal Justice Reform

Another area of controversy surrounding Biden is his role in the passage of the 1994 Crime Bill. While the bill aimed to address rising crime rates, it has been criticized for its contribution to mass incarceration, particularly affecting minority communities. Critics argue that the bill disproportionately targeted and punished individuals from marginalized backgrounds, leading to the over-policing and over-incarceration of non-violent offenders.

Biden's support for the Crime Bill has been a point of contention, especially in light of the ongoing calls for criminal justice reform. Many argue that his stance on the issue reflects a lack of understanding and empathy for the systemic issues that contribute to crime and the need for rehabilitation rather than punishment. This controversy has led to questions about Biden's commitment to racial justice and his ability to address the deep-rooted problems within the criminal justice system.

3.3.3 Anita Hill and Clarence Thomas Confirmation

During the confirmation hearings for Supreme Court Justice Clarence Thomas in 1991, Biden, as the chairman of the Senate Judiciary Committee, faced criticism for his handling of Anita Hill's sexual harassment allegations against Thomas. Many argue that Biden failed to adequately support and protect Hill during the hearings, allowing for a hostile environment that undermined her credibility and perpetuated a culture of disbelief towards survivors of sexual harassment.

Biden's role in the Anita Hill hearings has been a source of controversy, particularly in the context of the #MeToo movement and the increased focus on addressing sexual misconduct. Critics argue that his actions during the hearings reflect a lack of sensitivity and understanding towards the experiences of survivors, raising questions about his commitment to gender equality and his ability to address issues of sexual harassment and assault.

3.3.4 Flip-Flopping on Key Issues

Biden has faced criticism for his tendency to change his stance on key issues over the course of his political career. From his position on the Iraq War to his views on criminal justice reform and even his stance on abortion, Biden has been accused of political opportunism and a lack of consistency. Critics argue that these shifts in position raise doubts about his authenticity and his ability to stand firm on important matters.

This controversy surrounding Biden's flip-flopping on key issues has led to concerns about his trustworthiness and his ability to lead with conviction. It has also fueled skepticism about the sincerity of his campaign promises and his commitment to following through on his policy proposals.

In conclusion, Joseph Biden's political career has been marred by controversies and criticisms. From his involvement with Ukraine and Burisma to his role in the passage of the Crime Bill, his handling of the Anita Hill hearings, and his tendency to change positions on key issues, Biden has faced scrutiny and backlash throughout his journey. These controversies raise questions about his ethics, transparency, commitment to justice, and consistency as a political leader.

3.4 Legacy as Vice President

As Joseph Biden assumed the role of Vice President of the United States under President Barack Obama, many Americans had high hopes for his tenure. Biden had a long and storied political career, and his experience and knowledge were expected to contribute to the success of the Obama administration. However, as time went on, it became clear that Biden's legacy as Vice President would be marred by controversies, criticisms, and a lack of significant achievements.

One of the key aspects of Biden's legacy as Vice President was his role in shaping foreign policy and international relations. While he was often praised for his diplomatic skills and ability to build relationships with foreign leaders, his actual impact on U.S. foreign policy was questionable. Biden's approach to international affairs was often criticized for being too cautious and lacking a clear strategic vision. His handling of the Syrian civil war, for example, was seen by many as indecisive and ineffective, allowing the conflict to escalate and leading to a humanitarian crisis.

Another significant aspect of Biden's legacy as Vice President was the controversies and criticisms that surrounded him. One of the most notable controversies was his involvement in the Obama administration's handling of the Benghazi attack in 2012. Critics argued that Biden and the administration failed to adequately respond to the attack and provide proper security for the U.S. consulate in Libya. The incident raised questions about Biden's leadership and ability to handle crises effectively.

Additionally, Biden faced criticism for his role in the Obama administration's drone strike program. While the program was intended to target and eliminate high-value terrorist targets, it also resulted in the deaths of innocent civilians. Critics argued that Biden and the administration did not do enough to ensure the accuracy and legality of the strikes, leading to unnecessary loss of life and undermining the United States' moral standing in the world.

Despite these controversies and criticisms, Biden's legacy as Vice President also included some notable achievements. He played a key role in the passage of the Affordable Care Act, also known as Obamacare, which aimed to expand access to healthcare for millions of Americans. Biden's advocacy for the legislation helped secure its passage, although the law itself remained highly controversial and faced ongoing challenges.

Furthermore, Biden's legacy as Vice President also included his efforts to address issues such as gun control and violence against women. He was a vocal advocate for stricter gun control measures, particularly in the wake of mass shootings that occurred during his time in office. Biden also championed the reauthorization of the Violence Against Women Act, which aimed to protect women from domestic violence and provide support for survivors.

However, despite these achievements, Biden's legacy as Vice President was overshadowed by the lack of significant accomplishments and the controversies that surrounded him. Many critics argued that Biden failed to deliver on his promises and lacked the leadership and vision necessary to make a lasting impact. His tenure as Vice President was marked by a sense of missed opportunities and a lack of decisive action on key issues.

In conclusion, Joseph Biden's legacy as Vice President was a mixed bag of controversies, criticisms, and limited achievements. While he played a role in shaping foreign policy and addressing important domestic issues, his tenure was marred by controversies such as the Benghazi attack and the drone strike program. Biden's lack of significant accomplishments and his cautious approach to leadership left many questioning his effectiveness as Vice President. As he transitioned into the role of President, these concerns would continue to shape the perception of his political career and the future of America.

4 Presidential Campaign

4.1 Biden's Presidential Campaign

Joseph Biden's presidential campaign was marked by promises of hope, unity, and a return to normalcy. After serving as Vice President under Barack Obama, Biden presented himself as a seasoned politician with the experience and leadership necessary to guide the nation through challenging times. However, as his campaign unfolded, it became clear that Biden's promises were nothing more than empty rhetoric.

4.1.1 Promises of Change

During his campaign, Biden made a series of promises that resonated with many Americans. He pledged to address the pressing issues facing the country, such as healthcare, climate change, and racial inequality. Biden promised to expand the Affordable Care Act, invest in clean energy, and promote social justice. These promises appealed to a wide range of voters who were eager for change and believed that Biden would deliver on his commitments.

4.1.2 Lack of Transparency

Despite his promises of transparency, Biden's campaign was marred by a lack of openness and accountability. He avoided answering tough questions from the media and often provided vague or evasive responses. This lack of transparency raised concerns among voters who were looking for a leader who would be honest and forthright.

4.1.3 Flip-Flopping on Key Issues

Throughout his campaign, Biden demonstrated a tendency to flip-flop on key issues. He changed his stance on topics such as healthcare, criminal justice reform, and immigration, leaving voters unsure of where he truly stood. This inconsistency raised doubts about Biden's authenticity and his ability to follow through on his promises.

4.1.4 The Decline of America

Despite Biden's promises of a brighter future, his presidency has been marked by a decline in America's standing on the world stage. His weak foreign policy decisions and lack of leadership have allowed other nations to take advantage of the United States. From the disastrous withdrawal from Afghanistan to the strained relationships with key allies, Biden's presidency has left America vulnerable and diminished.

4.1.5 Border Crises and Immigration

One of the most pressing issues during Biden's campaign was the crisis at the southern border. He promised to address immigration reform in a humane and effective manner. However, his policies have resulted in a surge of illegal border crossings and overwhelmed border patrol agents. The lack of a coherent immigration strategy has not only put national security at risk but has also strained resources and created a humanitarian crisis.

4.1.6 Inflation and Economic Policies

Another area where Biden's campaign promises have fallen short is the economy. He pledged to build back better and create jobs for Americans. However, his economic policies, including massive government spending and proposed tax increases, have contributed to skyrocketing inflation and a struggling job market. The rising cost of goods and services has hit American families hard, eroding their purchasing power and undermining their financial stability.

4.1.7 Lack of Accountability

Throughout his campaign and presidency, Biden has shown a lack of accountability for his actions. He has repeatedly deflected blame onto others and refused to take responsibility for the consequences of his decisions. This lack of accountability has further eroded public trust in his leadership and raised questions about his ability to effectively govern.

4.1.8 The House Committee Investigations

The House Committee investigations have uncovered troubling evidence regarding Biden's family and their involvement in questionable business dealings. Allegations of corruption and nepotism have cast a shadow over his presidency and raised concerns about the integrity of his administration. The findings of these investigations have further fueled public skepticism and reinforced the perception that Biden's campaign promises were nothing more than empty words.

In conclusion, Biden's presidential campaign was characterized by promises of change and unity. However, his actions as president have failed to live up to these promises. From the decline of America's standing on the world stage to the border crises and inflation, Biden's presidency has been marked by a series of failures and broken commitments. The evidence uncovered by the House Committee investigations regarding his family's involvement in questionable business dealings only adds to the growing disillusionment with his leadership. It is clear that Biden's presidential campaign was a betrayal of the American people's trust and a missed opportunity for true change.

4.2 Campaign Promises

Joseph Biden's political career has been marked by a series of campaign promises that have ultimately proven to be empty and misleading. Throughout his various campaigns for public office, Biden has made grandiose pledges to the American people, promising to bring about positive change and address pressing issues facing the nation. However, upon closer examination, it becomes evident that these campaign promises were nothing more than political rhetoric designed to win over voters.

4.2.1 False Promises

One of the recurring themes in Joseph Biden's political career has been his propensity to make promises that he ultimately fails to deliver on. From his early years in the New Castle County Council to his presidential campaign, Biden has consistently made lofty pledges that have fallen flat. Whether it be his promises to tackle corruption, improve the economy, or address pressing social issues, Biden's track record of following through on his campaign promises is questionable at best.

4.2.2 Economic Policies

During his presidential campaign, Biden made numerous promises regarding economic policies that would supposedly benefit the American people. He pledged to create millions of new jobs, revitalize struggling industries, and promote economic growth. However, since taking office, the reality has been quite different. The implementation of Biden's economic policies has resulted in skyrocketing inflation, increased government spending, and a stagnant job market. The American people are now facing the consequences of these failed promises, with rising prices and a struggling economy.

4.2.3 Healthcare Reform

Another major campaign promise made by Biden was his commitment to healthcare reform. He vowed to build upon the Affordable Care Act and ensure that all Americans have access to affordable and quality healthcare. However, despite his promises, Biden has been unable to deliver on this front. The healthcare system remains burdened with high costs, limited access, and a lack of meaningful reform. Once again, Biden's campaign promise has proven to be nothing more than empty rhetoric.

4.2.4 Climate Change and Environmental Policies

Biden campaigned on a platform of addressing climate change and implementing environmentally friendly policies. He promised to rejoin the Paris Agreement, invest in renewable energy, and reduce carbon emissions. However, his actions since taking office have fallen short of these promises. The Biden administration's decision to cancel the Keystone XL pipeline and impose burdensome regulations on the energy industry has resulted in job losses and increased energy costs for American consumers. Once again, Biden's campaign promises have failed to materialize into meaningful action.

4.2.5 Immigration Reform

Perhaps one of the most controversial aspects of Biden's campaign promises was his commitment to immigration reform. He pledged to create a pathway to citizenship for undocumented immigrants, reform the immigration system, and address the humanitarian crisis at the border. However, since assuming office, the situation at the border has worsened, with a surge in illegal border crossings and overcrowded detention facilities. Biden's failure to effectively address the border crisis has raised questions about his ability to deliver on his campaign promises.

4.2.6 Criminal Justice Reform

Biden campaigned on a promise to address systemic racism and reform the criminal justice system. He vowed to end mass incarceration, promote police reform, and address racial disparities in the criminal justice system. However, his actions as president have fallen short of these promises. The Biden administration has been criticized for its handling of criminal justice issues, with concerns raised about its commitment to meaningful reform. Once again, Biden's campaign promises have proven to be hollow.

In conclusion, Joseph Biden's political career has been characterized by a series of campaign promises that have ultimately proven to be false and misleading. From economic policies to healthcare reform, climate change, immigration, and criminal justice, Biden's track record of delivering on his promises is questionable at best. The American people have been left to bear the consequences of these failed promises, with a declining economy, a struggling healthcare system, and a broken immigration system. It is clear that Biden's campaign promises were nothing more than empty rhetoric designed to win over voters, and the American people deserve better.

4.3 The Decline of America

Throughout Joseph Biden's political career, there has been a steady decline in the strength and prosperity of the United States. From his early years in the New Castle County Council to his current presidency, Biden's policies and actions have had a detrimental impact on the nation. This section will explore the various aspects of this decline, including the border crises, inflation, and the undermining of the United States on the international stage.

4.3.1 Border Crises and Immigration

One of the most pressing issues during Biden's presidency has been the border crises and the handling of immigration. Under his administration, there has been a significant surge in illegal border crossings, leading to overcrowded detention facilities and strained resources. The lack of effective border policies and enforcement has created a humanitarian crisis, with vulnerable individuals, including children, being subjected to dangerous conditions.

The Biden administration's approach to immigration has been marked by a disregard for the rule of law and a failure to address the root causes of migration. By rolling back key policies implemented by the previous administration, such as the Remain in Mexico policy and the construction of the border wall, Biden has sent a message of lax enforcement and open borders. This has not only incentivized illegal immigration but has also compromised national security by allowing potential threats to enter the country unchecked.

4.3.2 Inflation and Economic Policies

Another significant consequence of Biden's presidency has been the alarming rise in inflation and the negative impact on the economy. The administration's expansive spending policies, coupled with the Federal Reserve's loose monetary policy, have contributed to soaring prices across various sectors. Everyday essentials such as gas, groceries, and housing have become increasingly unaffordable for many Americans.

The excessive government spending, particularly through massive infrastructure bills and social programs, has raised concerns about the long-term sustainability of the economy. The burden of this spending will ultimately fall on future generations, saddling them with a staggering national debt and limited economic opportunities. Moreover, the inflationary pressures erode the purchasing power of the American people, further exacerbating the economic challenges faced by ordinary citizens.

4.3.3 Undermining the United States

On the international stage, Biden's foreign policy decisions have undermined the United States' standing and weakened its position as a global leader. From his approach to China to his handling of key alliances, Biden has demonstrated a lack of strategic foresight and a willingness to prioritize short-term gains over long-term national interests.

The Biden administration's soft stance on China, a country known for its human rights abuses and unfair trade practices, has raised concerns about the erosion of American values and the compromising of national security. By failing to hold China accountable for its actions, Biden has allowed the country to expand its influence and challenge the United States' position in the world.

Furthermore, the strained relationships with key allies, such as Israel and Saudi Arabia, have created a sense of uncertainty and weakened America's ability to effectively address global challenges. The lack of a coherent and consistent foreign policy approach has left many questioning the United States' commitment to its allies and its ability to lead on the world stage.

4.3.4 House Committee Investigations

In recent years, various House Committees have undertaken investigations into the Biden family's business dealings and the existence of shell corporations. These investigations have uncovered troubling evidence of potential corruption and nepotism within the Biden family. The revelations have raised serious questions about the integrity and ethics of Biden's political career.

The existence of shell corporations, which are often used to obscure financial transactions and hide potential conflicts of interest, has further eroded public trust in Biden's leadership. The lack of transparency and accountability surrounding these corporations raises concerns about the potential influence they may have had on Biden's decision-making process throughout his political career.

The findings of these House Committee investigations have had a significant impact on Biden's presidency, further tarnishing his reputation and credibility. The public perception of Biden's integrity and trustworthiness has been greatly diminished, leading to widespread backlash and calls for greater accountability.

In conclusion, Joseph Biden's political career has been marked by a decline in America's strength and prosperity. From the border crises and immigration challenges to the alarming rise in inflation and the undermining of the United States on the international stage, the consequences of his policies and actions have been detrimental to the nation. The evidence uncovered by House Committees regarding his family's business dealings and the existence of shell corporations has only further eroded public trust in his leadership. It is clear that the decline of America under Biden's presidency is a result of his misguided policies and a betrayal of the American people.

4.4 Border Crises and Immigration

The issue of border crises and immigration has been a significant challenge throughout Joseph Biden's political career. From his time as Vice President to his current presidency, Biden's approach to immigration policies has been a subject of controversy and criticism. This section will delve into the border crises that have unfolded under his leadership and the implications it has had on national security, humanitarian concerns, public opinion, and the response to these challenges.

4.4.1 The Border Policies and Crisis

Biden's approach to border policies has been marked by a significant shift from the previous administration. His promises of a more compassionate and inclusive approach to immigration have resulted in a surge of migrants attempting to enter the United States. The Biden administration's decision to reverse several immigration policies, such as the Migrant Protection Protocols (MPP) and the construction of the border wall, has created an environment that encourages illegal immigration.

As a result, the southern border has experienced a significant increase in the number of individuals attempting to cross illegally. The overwhelmed border patrol agents have struggled to manage the influx of migrants, leading to overcrowded detention facilities and a strain on resources. The lack of a comprehensive and effective immigration plan has exacerbated the border crisis, leaving both migrants and border patrol agents in a precarious situation.

4.4.2 Humanitarian Concerns

The border crises under Biden's presidency have raised serious humanitarian concerns. The surge of migrants, including unaccompanied minors, has put a strain on the capacity of detention facilities and the ability to provide adequate care for those in need. The conditions in these facilities have been widely criticized, with reports of overcrowding, unsanitary conditions, and limited access to medical care.

The Biden administration's failure to address these humanitarian concerns adequately has drawn criticism from both sides of the political spectrum. Advocacy groups and human rights organizations have called for immediate action to ensure the safety and well-being of migrants, particularly vulnerable populations such as children and families.

4.4.3 National Security Implications

The border crises and the influx of undocumented immigrants have significant national security implications. The lack of effective border control measures allows for the potential entry of individuals with criminal backgrounds or ties to terrorist organizations. This poses a threat to the safety and security of the United States and its citizens.

Additionally, the strain on border patrol resources and the diversion of their attention to managing the influx of migrants can potentially compromise their ability to address other national security concerns. The focus on managing the border crises has the potential to divert resources and attention away from other critical areas, such as drug trafficking and preventing the entry of illicit goods.

4.4.4 Public Opinion and Response

The border crises and the handling of immigration policies have had a significant impact on public opinion. The surge of migrants and the challenges faced at the border have fueled concerns among the American public regarding national security, economic impact, and the ability to effectively manage immigration.

Public opinion on immigration policies under the Biden administration has been divided. Supporters argue for a more compassionate and inclusive approach, emphasizing the need to address the root causes of migration and provide a pathway to citizenship for undocumented immigrants. On the other hand, critics argue that the lack of effective border control measures and the failure to address the border crises adequately undermine national security and the rule of law.

The response to the border crises has varied among different stakeholders. Some states and local governments have taken measures to address the challenges independently, while others have called for federal intervention and a more robust approach to border control. The public's response to the border crises has also influenced political discourse and policy debates surrounding immigration reform.

In conclusion, the border crises and immigration policies under Joseph Biden's political career have been a subject of controversy and criticism. The surge of migrants, overcrowded detention facilities, and strained resources have raised significant concerns about national security, humanitarian issues, and the ability to effectively manage immigration. The public's response to these challenges has shaped the political discourse surrounding immigration reform and highlighted the need for comprehensive and effective border control measures.

5 The Biden Presidency

5.1 Inflation and Economic Policies

One of the most pressing issues facing the United States under the Biden presidency is the alarming rise in inflation and the questionable economic policies implemented by the administration. Inflation, the sustained increase in the general price level of goods and services in an economy over time, has reached levels not seen in decades. This has had a detrimental impact on the American people, eroding their purchasing power and causing financial hardships for many.

The Biden administration's economic policies have been characterized by excessive government spending, which has contributed to the inflationary pressures. The massive stimulus packages, such as the American Rescue Plan and the proposed infrastructure bill, have injected trillions of dollars into the economy, leading to an oversupply of money. This influx of money has fueled demand, driving up prices for essential goods and services.

Furthermore, the administration's approach to monetary policy has raised concerns among economists and financial experts. The Federal Reserve, under the guidance of Chairman Jerome Powell, has maintained an accommodative stance, keeping interest rates low and continuing to purchase government bonds. While these measures were initially implemented to stimulate economic growth and mitigate the impact of the COVID-19 pandemic, they have inadvertently contributed to the inflationary pressures.

The consequences of inflation are far-reaching and affect all segments of society. Everyday Americans are feeling the pinch as the prices of essential goods, such as food, housing, and fuel, continue to rise. The cost of living has skyrocketed, making it increasingly difficult for families to make ends meet. Small businesses, already struggling to recover from the economic downturn caused by the pandemic, are facing additional challenges as they grapple with higher operating costs.

Inflation also erodes the value of savings and investments. Individuals who have diligently saved for retirement or other long-term goals find that their hard-earned money is losing its purchasing power. This not only undermines the financial security of individuals but also has broader implications for the overall economy.

Moreover, inflation has a regressive impact on society, disproportionately affecting low-income individuals and marginalized communities. Those who are already struggling to make ends meet are hit the hardest by rising prices, exacerbating income inequality and widening the wealth gap.

The Biden administration's response to the inflation crisis has been inadequate and lacking in transparency. Rather than addressing the root causes of inflation, the administration has downplayed its significance and attempted to shift the blame onto external factors, such as supply chain disruptions and global economic conditions. This lack of accountability and failure to implement effective measures to combat inflation further undermines the trust and confidence of the American people.

The consequences of inflation and misguided economic policies extend beyond the immediate impact on individuals and businesses. They have broader implications for the long-term stability and prosperity of the United States. Inflation erodes the value of the dollar, making it less attractive to foreign investors and weakening the country's position in the global economy. It also undermines the credibility of the Federal Reserve and raises concerns about the sustainability of the current economic trajectory.

The American people deserve a government that prioritizes responsible economic policies and takes decisive action to address the inflation crisis. It is imperative that the Biden administration reassess its approach to fiscal and monetary policy, focusing on measures that promote sustainable economic growth and protect the financial well-being of all Americans.

In conclusion, the alarming rise in inflation and the questionable economic policies implemented by the Biden administration have had a detrimental impact on the American people. Excessive government spending, accommodative monetary policy, and a lack of accountability have contributed to the inflationary pressures and eroded the purchasing power of individuals and businesses. It is crucial that the administration takes immediate and effective action to address the root causes of inflation and restore economic stability for the benefit of all Americans.

5.2 Undermining the United States

Throughout his political career, Joseph Biden has consistently demonstrated a pattern of undermining the United States and its interests. From his early years in politics to his current presidency, Biden's actions and policies have had detrimental effects on the nation. This section will delve into some of the key ways in which Biden has undermined the United States.

5.2.1 Weakening National Security

One of the most critical aspects of any presidency is ensuring the safety and security of the nation. However, Biden's decisions and policies have raised concerns about the weakening of national security. From his mishandling of the withdrawal from Afghanistan to his lax approach towards border security, Biden has left the United States vulnerable to potential threats.

The chaotic withdrawal from Afghanistan not only resulted in the loss of American lives but also allowed the Taliban to regain control, jeopardizing the progress made over the past two decades. This hasty and poorly executed decision sent a message to the world that the United States is unreliable and lacks strategic planning.

Furthermore, Biden's approach to border security has created a crisis that threatens national security. By rolling back many of the immigration policies put in place by the previous administration, Biden has effectively opened the floodgates, allowing illegal immigrants to enter the country unchecked. This not only poses a risk in terms of potential criminal activity but also strains resources and undermines the rule of law.

5.2.2 Undermining Foreign Policy

Another area where Biden has undermined the United States is in his approach to foreign policy. Rather than prioritizing American interests and maintaining strong alliances, Biden has often taken actions that appease other nations at the expense of the United States.

One example of this is his decision to reenter the Paris Climate Agreement without negotiating better terms for the United States. By doing so, Biden effectively committed the country to costly environmental regulations without ensuring that other major polluters, such as China, would also be held accountable. This puts American businesses at a disadvantage and undermines the country's economic competitiveness.

Additionally, Biden's approach to China has been concerning. Despite the well-documented human rights abuses and unfair trade practices carried out by the Chinese government, Biden has been hesitant to take a strong stance. This reluctance to confront China not only undermines the United States' position as a global leader but also puts American workers and industries at a disadvantage.

5.2.3 Economic Mismanagement

Biden's economic policies have also contributed to the undermining of the United States. His massive government spending initiatives, such as the American Rescue Plan and the proposed infrastructure bill, have raised concerns about the long-term sustainability of the economy.

By increasing government spending and proposing significant tax hikes, Biden risks stifling economic growth and burdening future generations with unsustainable levels of debt. Furthermore, his approach to inflation has been dismissive, downplaying its impact on everyday Americans. This lack of concern for rising prices and the erosion of purchasing power undermines the financial stability of American families.

5.2.4 Lack of Transparency and Accountability

One of the most troubling aspects of Biden's presidency is the lack of transparency and accountability surrounding his family's business dealings.

The House Committee has uncovered evidence that raises serious questions about potential corruption and nepotism within the Biden family.

Reports of Hunter Biden's involvement with foreign entities and the establishment of shell corporations have raised concerns about the potential for undue influence and conflicts of interest. The lack of transparency and the Biden administration's refusal to address these allegations only further erode public trust and confidence in the government.

The evidence uncovered by the House Committee warrants a thorough investigation to determine the extent of any wrongdoing and to hold those responsible accountable. The American people deserve transparency and honesty from their elected officials, and the failure to address these concerns undermines the very foundations of democracy.

In conclusion, Joseph Biden's political career has been marked by a consistent pattern of undermining the United States. From weakening national security to undermining foreign policy and mismanaging the economy, Biden's actions and policies have had detrimental effects on the nation. Furthermore, the lack of transparency and accountability surrounding his family's business dealings raises serious concerns about potential corruption. It is imperative that these issues are addressed and that the United States takes steps to rebuild and restore its standing on the global stage.

5.3 House Committee Investigations

The House Committee Investigations have played a crucial role in uncovering the truth behind Joseph Biden's political career. These investigations have shed light on the various controversies and scandals surrounding his family and their involvement in shell corporations. The evidence presented by the committee has revealed a web of deceit and corruption that has had far-reaching implications for the Biden presidency and the American people.

5.3.1 The Biden Family's Business Dealings

One of the key focuses of the House Committee Investigations has been the business dealings of the Biden family. The committee has delved into the intricate network of shell corporations and questionable financial transactions involving Hunter Biden, Joe Biden's son. These investigations have revealed a troubling pattern of influence peddling and potential conflicts of interest.

The evidence suggests that Hunter Biden used his father's position of power to secure lucrative business deals with foreign entities. These deals often raised concerns about the potential for foreign influence on American policy decisions. The committee has uncovered evidence of financial transactions involving countries such as China and Ukraine, raising questions about the integrity of the Biden family's business practices.

5.3.2 Nepotism and Favoritism

Another significant aspect of the House Committee Investigations has been the examination of nepotism and favoritism within the Biden administration. The evidence suggests that Joe Biden has used his position to benefit his family members, granting them access to influential positions and opportunities.

The committee has uncovered instances where Hunter Biden was appointed to lucrative positions despite his lack of qualifications or experience in the respective fields. These appointments raise concerns about the fairness and transparency of the Biden administration's decision-making process.

5.3.3 Impact on Biden's Presidency

The revelations brought forth by the House Committee Investigations have had a profound impact on the Biden presidency. The evidence of corruption and nepotism has eroded public trust in the administration and raised questions about the integrity of the decision-making process.

The investigations have also fueled concerns about the potential for foreign influence on American policy. The evidence of financial transactions involving foreign entities has raised questions about the extent to which the Biden administration may be compromised in its dealings with other nations.

Furthermore, the revelations have had political ramifications, with critics arguing that the Biden administration's focus should be on addressing these allegations rather than advancing its policy agenda. The investigations have become a significant distraction for the administration, diverting attention away from pressing issues facing the nation.

5.3.4 Public Perception and Backlash

The House Committee Investigations have had a significant impact on public perception of Joseph Biden and his political career. The evidence of corruption and questionable business dealings has led to a loss of trust and credibility in the eyes of many Americans.

Critics argue that the investigations have exposed a pattern of dishonesty and betrayal, undermining the image of Biden as a trustworthy and ethical leader. The revelations have fueled skepticism and cynicism among the public, further deepening the divide between supporters and detractors of the Biden administration.

The backlash against the Biden administration has been significant, with calls for further investigations and accountability. Many Americans believe that the evidence presented by the House Committee warrants a thorough examination and potential legal consequences for those involved.

In conclusion, the House Committee Investigations have played a crucial role in uncovering the truth behind Joseph Biden's political career. The evidence of corruption, nepotism, and questionable business dealings has had far-reaching implications for the Biden presidency and the American people. These investigations have eroded public trust, fueled political backlash, and raised concerns about the integrity of the decision-making process. The revelations brought forth by the committee have underscored the need for transparency, accountability, and a thorough examination of the allegations surrounding the Biden family and their involvement in shell corporations.

5.4 Family and Shell Corporations

Throughout Joseph Biden's political career, there have been numerous allegations and controversies surrounding his family's involvement in various business dealings and the use of shell corporations. These revelations have raised serious questions about potential conflicts of interest and ethical concerns. The House Committee's investigations have shed light on these matters, uncovering evidence that further exposes the extent of Biden's family and their involvement in questionable financial activities.

5.4.1 Hunter Biden's Business Ventures

One of the most prominent figures in the Biden family's business dealings is Hunter Biden, the president's son. Hunter Biden has been involved in several business ventures that have raised eyebrows and sparked investigations. These ventures include his position on the board of Ukrainian energy company Burisma Holdings, despite having no prior experience in the energy sector. The House Committee's findings have revealed that Hunter Biden's involvement with Burisma was highly questionable, with allegations of corruption and influence peddling.

Furthermore, the committee's investigations have also uncovered evidence of Hunter Biden's involvement in other international business dealings, particularly in China. It has been revealed that Hunter Biden had lucrative business arrangements with Chinese companies, raising concerns about potential conflicts of interest and the influence these relationships may have had on his father's political decisions.

5.4.2 Shell Corporations and Financial Transactions

In addition to Hunter Biden's business ventures, the House Committee's investigations have also focused on the Biden family's use of shell corporations and complex financial transactions. Shell corporations are legal entities that can be used to obscure the true ownership and control of assets, making it difficult to trace the flow of money and identify potential conflicts of interest.

The committee's findings have revealed that the Biden family utilized several shell corporations to conduct their financial affairs. These corporations were allegedly used to receive payments from foreign entities and engage in questionable financial transactions. The lack of transparency surrounding these transactions has raised concerns about potential illicit activities and the potential for foreign influence on the Biden family.

5.4.3 Conflicts of Interest and Ethical Concerns

The revelations surrounding the Biden family's business dealings and the use of shell corporations have raised serious questions about conflicts of interest and ethical concerns. Critics argue that these activities create a perception of impropriety and raise doubts about the integrity of Joseph Biden's political career.

The House Committee's investigations have uncovered evidence suggesting that the Biden family's financial interests may have influenced the president's policy decisions. This raises concerns about whether the Biden administration's actions are driven by the best interests of the American people or by personal financial gain.

Furthermore, the lack of transparency surrounding the Biden family's financial affairs and the use of shell corporations undermines the public's trust in the integrity of the political system. It erodes confidence in the ability of elected officials to act in the best interests of the country and reinforces the perception that there is a separate set of rules for the political elite.

5.4.4 Implications for Biden's Presidency

The revelations surrounding the Biden family's business dealings and the use of shell corporations have significant implications for Joseph Biden's presidency. They raise questions about his ability to effectively govern and make decisions that are free from personal financial interests.

The House Committee's findings have the potential to damage the credibility and legitimacy of the Biden administration. They provide ammunition to critics who argue that Biden's presidency is tainted by corruption and conflicts of interest. This could undermine the administration's ability to implement its policy agenda and erode public support for its initiatives.

Furthermore, the revelations surrounding the Biden family's financial affairs and the use of shell corporations could have long-lasting consequences for the Democratic Party as a whole. They reinforce the perception that the party is beholden to special interests and that its leaders are more concerned with personal gain than with serving the American people.

In conclusion, the House Committee's investigations into the Biden family's business dealings and the use of shell corporations have uncovered evidence that raises serious questions about conflicts of interest and ethical concerns. These revelations have the potential to undermine the credibility of Joseph Biden's presidency and erode public trust in the political system. The implications of these findings are far-reaching and have the potential to shape the future of American politics.

6 The Truth Uncovered

6.1 House Committee Findings

The House Committee's findings regarding Joseph Biden's family and their involvement with shell corporations have shed light on a web of corruption and nepotism that has plagued his political career. These revelations have further deepened the concerns about the integrity and ethics of the Biden administration.

6.1.1 Nepotism and Cronyism

One of the most alarming aspects uncovered by the House Committee is the extent of nepotism and cronyism within the Biden family. It has become evident that Biden has used his position of power to benefit his family members, disregarding the principles of meritocracy and fair competition. The committee's investigation has revealed numerous instances where Biden's family members, including his son Hunter Biden, have been involved in questionable business dealings and have received preferential treatment due to their familial connections.

6.1.2 Financial Irregularities and Shell Corporations

The House Committee's findings have also exposed a complex network of shell corporations and financial irregularities associated with the Biden family. These shell corporations have been used to obscure financial transactions and potentially facilitate illicit activities. The committee's investigation has revealed a pattern of suspicious financial transactions involving Biden's family members, raising serious questions about their ethical conduct and potential conflicts of interest.

6.1.3 Influence Peddling and Foreign Interests

Another troubling aspect uncovered by the House Committee is the influence peddling and potential foreign interference in Biden's political career. The investigation has revealed instances where Biden's family members, particularly his son Hunter Biden, have leveraged their connections to the Biden name to secure lucrative business deals with foreign entities. These dealings raise concerns about the potential compromise of national security and the influence of foreign interests on Biden's decision-making.

6.1.4 Ethical Violations and Lack of Transparency

The House Committee's findings have also highlighted numerous ethical violations and a lack of transparency within the Biden administration. The investigation has revealed instances where Biden and his family members failed to disclose their financial interests and potential conflicts of interest, violating ethical guidelines and undermining public trust. The lack of transparency surrounding these financial dealings raises questions about the integrity and honesty of the Biden administration.

6.1.5 Implications for Biden's Presidency

The House Committee's findings have significant implications for Biden's presidency. They raise serious doubts about his ability to govern ethically and effectively. The revelations of corruption, nepotism, and financial irregularities within his family have tarnished Biden's reputation and cast a shadow over his administration. These findings have eroded public trust and confidence in his leadership, making it increasingly difficult for him to implement his policy agenda and gain bipartisan support.

Furthermore, the House Committee's findings have also fueled concerns about the potential compromise of national security and the influence of foreign interests on Biden's decision-making. The revelations of influence peddling and questionable business dealings involving his family members have raised questions about the extent to which Biden's decisions may be influenced by personal gain rather than the best interests of the American people.

6.1.6 Public Perception and Backlash

The House Committee's findings have not only had an impact on Biden's presidency but also on public perception and the level of backlash he has faced. The revelations of corruption and nepotism within his family have further polarized the American public, with critics arguing that Biden's actions are indicative of a broader culture of corruption within the political establishment.

The lack of transparency and ethical violations uncovered by the House Committee have also fueled skepticism and distrust among the American people. Many view these findings as evidence of a political elite that is out of touch with the concerns and needs of ordinary citizens. As a result, Biden's approval ratings have suffered, and he has faced significant criticism from both political opponents and disillusioned supporters.

In conclusion, the House Committee's findings regarding the Biden family's involvement with shell corporations and their questionable business dealings have exposed a troubling pattern of corruption and nepotism. These revelations have raised serious concerns about the integrity and ethics of the Biden administration, as well as the potential compromise of national security. The impact of these findings on Biden's presidency and public perception has been significant, eroding trust and fueling backlash. The full extent of the implications of these findings remains to be seen, but they undoubtedly cast a shadow over Biden's political career and legacy.

6.2 Corruption and Nepotism

Corruption and nepotism have long plagued the political career of Joseph Biden. From his early years in the New Castle County Council to his time as Vice President and now President of the United States, Biden's actions have raised serious concerns about his integrity and the ethical standards he upholds.

6.2.1 The Biden Family's Business Ventures

One of the most alarming revelations that the House Committee has uncovered is the involvement of the Biden family in questionable business ventures. Hunter Biden, the President's son, has been at the center of numerous controversies, particularly regarding his foreign business dealings. It has been revealed that Hunter Biden was involved in lucrative business arrangements in countries such as Ukraine and China, raising questions about potential conflicts of interest and the influence that these foreign entities may have had on the Biden family.

Furthermore, the establishment of shell corporations by the Biden family has raised suspicions of potential money laundering and tax evasion. These shell corporations, often located in offshore tax havens, have allowed the Biden family to shield their financial activities from public scrutiny. The lack of transparency surrounding these business dealings is deeply concerning and raises doubts about the integrity of the Biden family.

6.2.2 Nepotism and Favoritism

Nepotism has also been a recurring theme throughout Biden's political career. From his time as Vice President to his current presidency, Biden has shown a willingness to prioritize the interests of his family members over the well-being of the American people. This nepotistic behavior is exemplified by the appointment of Hunter Biden to the board of a Ukrainian energy company, despite his lack of experience in the energy sector. This appointment reeks of favoritism and raises questions about the extent to which Biden is willing to abuse his power for personal gain.

Additionally, Biden's decision to appoint family members to key positions within his administration has further fueled concerns about nepotism. For example, his nomination of his son-in-law, Howard Krein, to a prominent role in the COVID-19 response team has been met with criticism and accusations of cronyism. These actions not only undermine the principles of meritocracy and fair competition but also erode public trust in the integrity of the Biden administration.

6.2.3 Ethical Violations

The House Committee's findings have also shed light on several ethical violations committed by Biden and his family. For instance, it has been revealed that Hunter Biden failed to disclose his foreign business dealings on his tax returns, a clear violation of tax laws. This deliberate omission raises concerns about the Biden family's commitment to transparency and adherence to legal obligations.

Furthermore, the involvement of the Biden family in business dealings with foreign entities raises questions about potential conflicts of interest. The close ties between the Biden family and foreign governments or corporations create a situation where personal financial gain may influence policy decisions. This type of ethical compromise undermines the integrity of the presidency and erodes public trust in the government.

6.2.4 Implications for Biden's Presidency

The revelations of corruption and nepotism surrounding Biden and his family have significant implications for his presidency. They call into question his ability to lead with integrity and prioritize the interests of the American people above personal gain. The American public deserves a leader who is transparent, ethical, and free from the influence of special interests.

Moreover, these revelations have the potential to undermine Biden's credibility on the international stage. Foreign governments and leaders may view the Biden administration with skepticism, questioning the motivations behind its decisions and policies. This could have far-reaching consequences for America's standing in the world and its ability to effectively address global challenges.

6.2.5 Public Perception and Backlash

The exposure of corruption and nepotism within the Biden family has not gone unnoticed by the American public. Many citizens are deeply concerned about the ethical standards of their elected officials and the potential impact on the country's governance. The revelations have fueled a sense of disillusionment and mistrust among the electorate, further widening the divide between the government and the people.

The backlash against Biden's alleged corruption and nepotism has been significant. Calls for investigations and accountability have grown louder, with demands for transparency and a thorough examination of the Biden family's business dealings. The American people are demanding answers and holding their elected officials to account for their actions.

In conclusion, the evidence uncovered by the House Committee regarding corruption and nepotism within the Biden family is deeply troubling. It raises serious concerns about the integrity of Joseph Biden and his ability to lead with transparency and prioritize the interests of the American people. The implications for his presidency are significant, as they undermine his credibility both domestically and internationally. The public backlash against these revelations reflects a growing demand for accountability and a renewed commitment to ethical governance.

6.3 Impact on Biden's Presidency

Joseph Biden's presidency has been marked by a series of controversies and scandals that have had a significant impact on his administration. From the moment he took office, it became clear that the promises he made during his campaign were nothing more than empty rhetoric. The American people were promised a return to stability and prosperity, but instead, they have been met with a decline in America's standing both domestically and internationally.

6.3.1 Economic Policies and Inflation

One of the most pressing issues facing the Biden administration is the alarming rise in inflation. Despite promising to prioritize the economy and create jobs, Biden's economic policies have only exacerbated the problem. His massive government spending initiatives, such as the American Rescue Plan and the proposed infrastructure bill, have contributed to skyrocketing inflation rates. The cost of goods and services has increased, putting a strain on American families and businesses. This inflationary pressure has eroded the purchasing power of the American people and threatens the stability of the economy.

6.3.2 Undermining the United States

Another significant impact of Biden's presidency has been the undermining of the United States on the global stage. Through a series of foreign policy decisions, Biden has weakened America's position and damaged relationships with key allies. His approach to international relations has been marked by a lack of strategic vision and a prioritization of global agendas over American interests. This has resulted in a loss of credibility and influence, leaving the United States vulnerable to the ambitions of adversarial nations.

6.3.3 House Committee Investigations

The House Committee investigations into Biden's family and their involvement with shell corporations have shed light on the extent of corruption and nepotism within his administration. The evidence uncovered has raised serious questions about the ethical conduct of the president and his family members. The revelations have exposed a web of financial dealings that appear to have been used to enrich the Biden family at the expense of the American people. These investigations have further eroded public trust in the president and his ability to lead with integrity.

6.3.4 Public Perception and Backlash

The impact of Biden's presidency extends beyond policy failures and scandals. Public perception of his leadership has taken a significant hit, with many Americans expressing dissatisfaction and disillusionment. The promises of unity and bipartisanship have given way to a deeply divided nation, as Biden's policies and rhetoric have only served to further polarize the country. The lack of transparency and accountability within his administration has fueled public distrust and skepticism.

Furthermore, the media's role in shaping public perception cannot be overlooked. The biased and selective reporting by mainstream media outlets has shielded Biden from scrutiny and downplayed the severity of his failures. This media cover-up has contributed to a lack of awareness among the general public regarding the true impact of his presidency.

The backlash against Biden's policies and leadership has been evident in various forms. Protests and demonstrations have taken place across the country, with Americans voicing their discontent and frustration. The midterm elections saw a significant shift in political dynamics, with Republicans gaining seats and control in various state legislatures. This backlash is a clear indication that the American people are not satisfied with the direction in which Biden is taking the country.

In conclusion, the impact of Joseph Biden's presidency has been far-reaching and detrimental to the United States. From his economic policies and the rise in inflation to the undermining of America's global standing, the consequences of his leadership have been severe. The House Committee investigations into his family's financial dealings have only further tarnished his reputation and raised questions about his integrity. The public perception of his presidency has suffered, and the backlash against his policies has been significant. As the nation grapples with the consequences of his tenure, it is clear that rebuilding America will require a reevaluation of the failed policies and a commitment to true leadership.

6.4 Public Perception and Backlash

Public perception plays a crucial role in shaping the political landscape of any leader. It is the collective opinion of the people that can either make or break a politician's career. In the case of Joseph Biden, his political career has been marred by controversies, scandals, and a growing sense of betrayal among the American public.

6.4.1 Loss of Trust

One of the most significant factors contributing to the public backlash against Joseph Biden is the loss of trust. Throughout his political career, Biden has made numerous promises to the American people, only to break them time and time again. From his early years in the New Castle County Council to his tenure as Vice President and eventually President, Biden's false political promises have left a bitter taste in the mouths of many.

6.4.2 Broken Promises

Biden's political career has been characterized by a series of broken promises. Whether it was his pledge to tackle corruption and scandals during his time in the New Castle County Council or his assurance to bring about meaningful change during his presidential campaign, Biden has consistently failed to deliver on his commitments. This pattern of broken promises has eroded public trust and left many feeling disillusioned and betrayed.

6.4.3 Lack of Transparency

Another factor contributing to the public backlash against Biden is the perceived lack of transparency. Throughout his career, Biden has been accused of being secretive and evasive, particularly when it comes to his family's involvement in questionable business dealings. The recent revelations about his family and shell corporations have only further fueled public skepticism and raised concerns about potential conflicts of interest.

6.4.4 Growing Frustration

The American public's frustration with Biden's political career has been steadily growing. Many feel that he has prioritized his own interests and the interests of his inner circle over the needs of the American people. From his controversial legislative record to his questionable foreign policy decisions, Biden's actions have often been seen as self-serving and disconnected from the concerns of everyday Americans.

6.4.5 Polarizing Figure

Biden's presidency has also contributed to the polarization of the American public. His policies and actions have drawn sharp criticism from both sides of the political spectrum, further deepening the divide in the country. Whether it is his handling of the border crisis or his economic policies that have led to skyrocketing inflation, Biden's decisions have been met with strong opposition and have fueled the flames of political discord.

6.4.6 Media Bias and Cover-ups

The role of the media in shaping public perception cannot be underestimated. However, many argue that the media has been complicit in covering up Biden's shortcomings and downplaying the controversies surrounding his political career. Selective reporting and manipulation of information have further contributed to the public's growing distrust of both Biden and the media.

6.4.7 Backlash and Consequences

The public backlash against Biden has had significant consequences for his presidency. It has not only damaged his credibility but has also hindered his ability to effectively govern. The lack of public trust has made it difficult for Biden to garner support for his policies and initiatives, leading to a gridlocked political environment and a divided nation.

6.4.8 The Future of Biden's Political Career

As the public perception of Biden continues to sour, the future of his political career remains uncertain. The mounting backlash and loss of trust have cast a shadow over his ability to lead effectively. Whether he can regain the public's trust and overcome the challenges he faces will ultimately determine the trajectory of his political career.

In conclusion, the public perception and backlash against Joseph Biden have been fueled by broken promises, a lack of transparency, growing frustration, and a polarizing presidency. The media's role in shaping public opinion and the consequences of the public's disillusionment have further compounded the challenges Biden faces. The future of his political career hangs in the balance as he grapples with the fallout of his actions and attempts to rebuild public trust.

7 The Media's Role

7.1 Media's Treatment of Biden

Throughout Joseph Biden's political career, the media has played a significant role in shaping public perception and influencing the narrative surrounding his actions and decisions. However, it is essential to examine the media's treatment of Biden critically, as it has often been characterized by bias and cover-ups.

7.1.1 Selective Reporting

One of the most concerning aspects of the media's treatment of Biden is its tendency towards selective reporting. Rather than providing objective and comprehensive coverage, certain media outlets have chosen to focus on specific aspects of Biden's career while ignoring or downplaying others.

For example, during Biden's vice presidency, the media often highlighted his role in foreign policy and international relations, portraying him as a seasoned statesman. However, they conveniently overlooked controversies and criticisms surrounding his foreign policy decisions, such as the handling of the Benghazi attack or the Obama administration's approach to Syria.

Similarly, during Biden's presidential campaign, the media selectively reported on his campaign promises, often presenting them in a favorable light without thoroughly scrutinizing their feasibility or potential consequences. This biased reporting created a distorted image of Biden as a competent and trustworthy leader, while neglecting to address the potential pitfalls of his proposed policies.

7.1.2 Manipulation of Information

Another concerning aspect of the media's treatment of Biden is its manipulation of information to fit a particular narrative. Rather than presenting the facts objectively, some media outlets have engaged in cherry-picking, distortion, and even outright misinformation to shape public opinion.

For instance, during Biden's presidency, the media has often downplayed or dismissed concerns regarding inflation and its impact on the economy. Instead of providing a comprehensive analysis of the causes and consequences of rising prices, some media outlets have chosen to focus on other issues or downplay the significance of inflation altogether. This manipulation of information prevents the public from fully understanding the economic challenges facing the country.

Furthermore, the media's manipulation of information extends to issues such as border crises and immigration. Rather than providing an unbiased assessment of the situation, some media outlets have portrayed Biden's border policies as compassionate and humanitarian, while neglecting to address the national security implications and the strain it puts on local communities. This manipulation of information prevents a comprehensive understanding of the complex issues at hand.

7.1.3 Consequences of Media Bias

The consequences of media bias in the treatment of Biden are far-reaching and have significant implications for the democratic process and the public's ability to make informed decisions. When the media fails to provide objective and comprehensive coverage, it undermines the public's trust in the information they receive and distorts their understanding of political events and figures.

Media bias also perpetuates a divisive political climate by reinforcing existing partisan divides. When certain media outlets consistently present a one-sided view of Biden's actions and decisions, it further polarizes the public and hinders constructive dialogue and debate.

Moreover, media bias in the treatment of Biden undermines the media's role as a watchdog and a check on political power. The media has a responsibility to hold politicians accountable and provide the public with accurate and unbiased information. When this responsibility is compromised, it weakens the democratic process and allows for potential abuses of power to go unchecked.

In conclusion, the media's treatment of Joseph Biden throughout his political career has been characterized by bias and cover-ups. Selective reporting, manipulation of information, and the consequences of media bias have all contributed to a distorted narrative surrounding Biden's actions and decisions. It is crucial for the public to critically evaluate the information they receive and seek out diverse and objective sources to form a comprehensive understanding of Biden's political career.

7.2 Selective Reporting

Selective reporting is a tactic often employed by the media to shape public opinion and control the narrative surrounding a particular individual or event. In the case of Joseph Biden's political career, selective reporting has played a significant role in shielding him from scrutiny and downplaying the numerous controversies and scandals that have plagued his tenure.

One of the most glaring examples of selective reporting is the media's treatment of Biden's involvement in corruption and nepotism. Despite mounting evidence and credible allegations, the mainstream media has largely ignored or downplayed these serious accusations. The House Committee's findings regarding Biden's family and their involvement in shell corporations have been conveniently swept under the rug, with little to no coverage from major news outlets.

This selective reporting not only shields Biden from accountability but also undermines the public's right to know the truth about their elected officials. By cherry-picking which stories to cover and which to ignore, the media manipulates the information available to the public, creating a distorted perception of reality.

Furthermore, the media's bias in favor of Biden is evident in their portrayal of his policies and actions. Positive aspects of his presidency are often highlighted, while negative consequences are downplayed or ignored altogether. This biased reporting creates a false narrative that paints Biden as a competent and effective leader, despite mounting evidence to the contrary.

For example, the media has largely ignored the economic challenges and impact of Biden's policies, particularly the issue of inflation. Rising prices and a weakened economy have become a reality for many Americans, yet the media has failed to adequately report on the causes and consequences of this crisis. By omitting this crucial information, the media shields Biden from criticism and prevents the public from fully understanding the economic challenges they face.

Selective reporting also extends to Biden's foreign policy decisions and their implications for America's standing in the world. The media often portrays Biden as a skilled diplomat and a champion of international cooperation, while downplaying the negative consequences of his actions. This biased reporting not only distorts the public's perception of Biden's foreign policy but also prevents a comprehensive understanding of the potential risks and dangers associated with his decisions.

The consequences of selective reporting are far-reaching and detrimental to the democratic process. When the media fails to provide accurate and unbiased information, the public is left uninformed and unable to make informed decisions. This lack of transparency erodes trust in the media and undermines the foundations of a functioning democracy.

Moreover, selective reporting perpetuates a culture of impunity among politicians, allowing them to evade accountability for their actions. When the media fails to hold elected officials to account, it sends a message that they can act with impunity, free from scrutiny or consequences. This not only undermines the principles of justice and fairness but also erodes public trust in the political system as a whole.

In conclusion, selective reporting has played a significant role in shaping the narrative surrounding Joseph Biden's political career. By downplaying or ignoring controversies and scandals, the media has shielded Biden from accountability and prevented the public from fully understanding the true nature of his actions. This biased reporting undermines the democratic process and erodes public trust in the media and the political system. It is crucial for the public to seek out diverse and reliable sources of information to ensure a more comprehensive understanding of the issues at hand.

7.3 Manipulation of Information

Throughout Joseph Biden's political career, one recurring theme has been the manipulation of information. Whether it was during his time as Vice President or his current presidency, Biden and his administration have consistently used various tactics to control the narrative and shape public opinion. This manipulation of information has had far-reaching consequences for the American people and the integrity of the democratic process.

7.3.1 Controlling the Narrative

One of the most common tactics used by the Biden administration to manipulate information is through controlling the narrative. This involves carefully crafting and disseminating messages that align with their political agenda while suppressing or downplaying any information that may be detrimental to their image. By controlling the narrative, they can shape public opinion and control the discourse surrounding important issues.

The mainstream media plays a significant role in this manipulation of information. Rather than providing unbiased reporting, many media outlets have become mouthpieces for the Biden administration, amplifying their messages and suppressing dissenting voices. This selective reporting further reinforces the administration's narrative and prevents the public from receiving a balanced view of the facts.

7.3.2 Misleading Statistics and Data

Another tactic employed by the Biden administration is the use of misleading statistics and data. By selectively presenting information or cherry-picking data, they can create a false impression of success or downplay the severity of certain issues. This manipulation of statistics is particularly evident in areas such as the economy, immigration, and crime rates.

For example, when it comes to the economy, the administration often highlights positive indicators such as stock market performance or job growth while ignoring the rising inflation and increasing national debt. By focusing on the positive aspects and downplaying the negative consequences of their policies, they create a distorted perception of the overall economic situation.

Similarly, in the context of immigration, the administration has been known to manipulate data to downplay the severity of the border crisis. By selectively presenting statistics that show a decrease in border apprehensions or emphasizing the number of individuals processed legally, they create the illusion of effective border control while ignoring the overwhelming influx of illegal immigrants.

7.3.3 Suppressing Dissenting Voices

In addition to controlling the narrative and manipulating data, the Biden administration has also been accused of suppressing dissenting voices. This includes silencing or discrediting individuals or organizations that criticize their policies or present alternative viewpoints. By marginalizing dissent, they can maintain a monopoly on the information available to the public and prevent any challenges to their narrative.

One notable example of this is the censorship of conservative voices on social media platforms. Many individuals and organizations that express conservative or dissenting views have been deplatformed or had their content restricted, effectively silencing their voices and limiting the diversity of perspectives available to the public.

7.3.4 Consequences of Manipulation

The manipulation of information by the Biden administration has had significant consequences for the American people and the democratic process. By controlling the narrative and manipulating data, they undermine the public's ability to make informed decisions and hold the government accountable. This erosion of transparency and trust in the government has far-reaching implications for the functioning of a democratic society.

Furthermore, the manipulation of information perpetuates a cycle of misinformation and disinformation, making it increasingly difficult for the public to discern the truth. This not only hinders public discourse but also creates divisions within society as individuals become entrenched in their own echo chambers of information.

Ultimately, the manipulation of information by the Biden administration undermines the principles of transparency, accountability, and democracy. It is essential for the American people to be aware of these tactics and actively seek out diverse sources of information to ensure a well-informed citizenry capable of holding their elected officials accountable. Only through a commitment to truth and transparency can the democratic process thrive and the American people be truly empowered.

7.4 Consequences of Media Bias

The media plays a crucial role in shaping public opinion and providing information to the masses. In a democratic society, it is expected that the media will act as a watchdog, holding those in power accountable and providing unbiased reporting. However, in recent years, media bias has become a significant concern, with many outlets accused of favoring certain political ideologies or individuals.

7.4.1 Manipulation of Information

One of the most significant consequences of media bias is the manipulation of information. When the media is biased, it selectively reports on certain events or issues, often omitting crucial details or presenting them in a way that supports a particular narrative. This manipulation of information can lead to a distorted view of reality and prevent the public from making informed decisions.

In the case of Joseph Biden's political career, media bias has played a significant role in shaping public perception. Certain media outlets have been accused of downplaying or ignoring allegations of corruption and scandals surrounding Biden, while simultaneously amplifying negative stories about his political opponents. This selective reporting has created an uneven playing field, where the public is not presented with a complete picture of Biden's actions and decisions.

7.4.2 Lack of Accountability

Media bias also contributes to a lack of accountability for those in power. When the media fails to hold politicians accountable for their actions, it undermines the democratic process and erodes public trust. In the case of Joseph Biden, media bias has shielded him from scrutiny, allowing him to avoid answering tough questions or addressing allegations of wrongdoing.

The lack of accountability resulting from media bias has far-reaching consequences. It allows politicians to act with impunity, knowing that they will not face significant backlash or consequences for their actions. This lack of accountability undermines the principles of democracy and can lead to a culture of corruption and abuse of power.

7.4.3 Polarization and Divisions

Media bias also contributes to the polarization and divisions within society. When the media presents a one-sided view of political events and issues, it reinforces existing biases and prevents meaningful dialogue and understanding between different groups. This polarization can lead to increased hostility and a breakdown of civil discourse.

In the case of Joseph Biden's political career, media bias has contributed to the deep divisions within society. Supporters of Biden often dismiss any criticism or allegations against him as mere political attacks, while his opponents feel frustrated and unheard. This polarization prevents constructive dialogue and hinders the ability to find common ground and solutions to pressing issues.

7.4.4 Erosion of Trust in the Media

Perhaps one of the most significant consequences of media bias is the erosion of trust in the media itself. When the public perceives the media as biased and untrustworthy, it undermines the essential role that the media plays in a democratic society. Trust in the media is crucial for a well-informed citizenry and a functioning democracy.

The bias in media coverage of Joseph Biden's political career has led to a growing skepticism and distrust among the public. Many people feel that they cannot rely on the media to provide them with accurate and unbiased information. This erosion of trust further exacerbates the divisions within society and undermines the democratic process.

7.4.5 Impact on Democracy

Media bias has far-reaching consequences for democracy as a whole. When the media fails to provide unbiased reporting, it undermines the ability of the public to make informed decisions and hold those in power accountable. A well-functioning democracy relies on a free and independent media that acts as a check on government power.

In the case of Joseph Biden's political career, media bias has hindered the public's ability to fully assess his actions and decisions. The lack of critical reporting and the manipulation of information have prevented the public from understanding the full extent of Biden's involvement in corruption and scandals. This lack of transparency undermines the democratic process and erodes public trust in the political system.

In conclusion, media bias has significant consequences for the political career of Joseph Biden and for democracy as a whole. The manipulation of information, lack of accountability, polarization, erosion of trust, and impact on democracy are all direct results of media bias. It is essential for the media to uphold its responsibility to provide unbiased reporting and hold those in power accountable to ensure a well-informed citizenry and a functioning democracy.

8 The Decline of America

8.1 Foreign Policy Failures

Foreign policy is a crucial aspect of any nation's governance, as it shapes a country's relationships with other nations and influences its standing in the global arena. Unfortunately, Joseph Biden's political career has been marred by a series of foreign policy failures that have had far-reaching consequences for the United States. From his time as Vice President to his current presidency, Biden's decisions and actions have weakened America's position on the world stage and compromised its national security.

One of the most significant foreign policy failures of the Biden administration has been its handling of the withdrawal of U.S. troops from Afghanistan. The abrupt and poorly executed withdrawal resulted in the rapid takeover of the country by the Taliban, leaving chaos and uncertainty in its wake. The hasty retreat not only endangered the lives of Afghan allies who had worked alongside American forces but also allowed for the resurgence of terrorist organizations such as ISIS-K. This failure not only damaged America's credibility but also posed a direct threat to national security.

Another foreign policy failure under Biden's leadership has been his approach to China. Despite the growing concerns about China's aggressive actions in the South China Sea, human rights abuses, and unfair trade practices, the Biden administration has failed to take a strong and decisive stance. Instead, Biden has adopted a conciliatory approach, hoping to engage China in dialogue and cooperation. However, this approach has only emboldened China, allowing it to continue its expansionist agenda and disregard international norms. By failing to confront China's actions, Biden has compromised America's interests and security in the Asia-Pacific region.

Furthermore, the Biden administration's reentry into the Iran nuclear deal, formally known as the Joint Comprehensive Plan of Action (JCPOA), has been widely criticized as a foreign policy failure. The JCPOA, negotiated during the Obama administration, aimed to curb Iran's nuclear program in exchange for sanctions relief. However, the deal was flawed and failed to address Iran's support for terrorism and destabilizing activities in the Middle East. By rejoining the JCPOA without demanding significant changes, Biden has effectively given Iran a lifeline, allowing it to continue its malign activities while receiving economic benefits.

Biden's approach to Russia has also been marked by failures. Despite Russia's continued aggression in Ukraine, cyberattacks on American infrastructure, and interference in democratic processes, the Biden administration has failed to take decisive action. The lack of a strong response has only emboldened Russian President Vladimir Putin, who continues to challenge American interests and undermine global stability. By failing to hold Russia accountable for its actions, Biden has sent a message of weakness and allowed Russia to act with impunity.

Moreover, Biden's decision to halt construction of the Keystone XL pipeline, a project that would have strengthened America's energy independence and created jobs, has damaged relations with Canada, one of America's closest allies. This decision not only undermined the economic interests of both countries but also sent a signal to other nations that America is willing to sacrifice its energy security for political reasons.

These foreign policy failures have had significant consequences for the United States. They have weakened America's position as a global leader, compromised its national security, and damaged its relationships with key allies. The lack of a coherent and effective foreign policy strategy under Biden's leadership has left the United States vulnerable to threats and diminished its ability to advance its interests on the world stage.

In conclusion, Joseph Biden's political career has been marred by a series of foreign policy failures that have had detrimental effects on the United States. From the mishandling of the withdrawal from Afghanistan to the failure to confront China, Iran, and Russia effectively, Biden's foreign policy decisions have weakened America's position in the world. These failures have compromised national security, damaged relationships with key allies, and undermined America's standing as a global leader. It is essential to assess and learn from these failures to ensure a more effective and robust foreign policy in the future.

8.2 National Security Concerns

National security is a paramount concern for any nation, as it encompasses the protection of its citizens, territory, and interests from external threats. In the case of Joseph Biden's political career, there have been significant concerns regarding his approach to national security and the potential consequences it may have for the United States.

8.2.1 Weakening Military Capabilities

One of the primary national security concerns during Biden's presidency has been the weakening of the United States' military capabilities. Despite the importance of maintaining a strong and well-equipped military, Biden's administration has made several decisions that have raised eyebrows and caused alarm among defense experts.

Firstly, the abrupt withdrawal of U.S. troops from Afghanistan without a comprehensive plan in place has had severe repercussions. The hasty withdrawal allowed the Taliban to regain control of the country, putting at risk the stability of the region and potentially providing a safe haven for terrorist organizations. This decision not only undermined the sacrifices made by American soldiers but also jeopardized the security of the United States and its allies.

Furthermore, Biden's proposed defense budget cuts have raised concerns about the readiness and preparedness of the U.S. military. Slashing defense spending at a time when global threats are on the rise sends a worrying message to adversaries and weakens the United States' ability to respond effectively to emerging challenges.

8.2.2 Neglecting Cybersecurity

In an increasingly interconnected world, cybersecurity has become a critical aspect of national security. However, Biden's approach to cybersecurity has been questionable at best. The recent surge in cyberattacks targeting American infrastructure, including the Colonial Pipeline and JBS Foods, has exposed vulnerabilities in the nation's cybersecurity defenses.

Despite these attacks, the Biden administration has failed to present a comprehensive strategy to address the growing threat of cyber warfare. The lack of a robust response not only puts critical infrastructure at risk but also undermines the United States' ability to protect its citizens and maintain its position as a global leader.

8.2.3 Immigration and Border Security

Another national security concern that has emerged during Biden's presidency is the issue of immigration and border security. The Biden administration's lax approach to immigration policies, particularly at the southern border, has raised significant concerns about national security.

By rolling back many of the immigration policies implemented by the previous administration, Biden has created a situation where illegal border crossings have surged to unprecedented levels. This influx of undocumented individuals poses potential security risks, as it becomes increasingly difficult to screen and vet those entering the country.

Additionally, the lack of effective border security measures allows for the potential entry of individuals with malicious intent, including criminals and even potential terrorists. This disregard for border security not only compromises national security but also undermines the rule of law and the integrity of the immigration system.

8.2.4 Weakening Alliances and Global Influence

Maintaining strong alliances and a robust global influence is crucial for the United States to effectively address global challenges and protect its national security interests. However, Biden's approach to international relations has raised concerns about the weakening of these alliances and the diminishing influence of the United States on the world stage.

Biden's decision to reenter the Paris Climate Agreement without securing meaningful concessions for the United States has been viewed by many as a sign of weakness. It sends a message to adversaries that the United States is willing to prioritize global agendas over its own national interests.

Furthermore, the strained relationship with key allies, such as Israel, has raised questions about the United States' commitment to its longstanding partnerships. Weakening these alliances not only undermines the United States' ability to address global challenges collectively but also leaves room for adversaries to exploit divisions and exert influence in regions of strategic importance.

In conclusion, national security concerns have been a significant aspect of Joseph Biden's political career. From the weakening of military capabilities to neglecting cybersecurity, and from lax immigration policies to the potential erosion of alliances and global influence, these concerns raise questions about the effectiveness of his approach to safeguarding the United States' national security interests. It is essential for policymakers and citizens alike to carefully evaluate these concerns and their potential long-term consequences for the future of America.

8.3 Economic Impact

The economic impact of Joseph Biden's political career cannot be ignored. Throughout his time in various positions of power, from the New Castle County Council to the Vice Presidency and now the Presidency, Biden's policies and decisions have had far-reaching consequences for the American economy. This section will delve into the economic impact of his tenure, examining the effects of his policies, the state of the economy under his leadership, and the implications for the future of America.

8.3.1 Economic Policies and Legislation

One of the key aspects of any political leader's impact on the economy is their economic policies and the legislation they enact. Biden's economic agenda has been marked by a significant increase in government spending and intervention. From the American Rescue Plan Act to the proposed infrastructure bill, his administration has sought to inject trillions of dollars into the economy. While these measures may have been intended to stimulate growth and address pressing issues, such as the COVID-19 pandemic, they have raised concerns about the long-term consequences of such massive spending.

Critics argue that the excessive government spending under Biden's leadership has the potential to fuel inflation, increase the national debt, and burden future generations with the consequences of unsustainable fiscal policies. The impact of these policies on the economy remains a subject of debate, with supporters pointing to short-term benefits such as job creation and economic recovery, while skeptics express concerns about the potential long-term consequences.

8.3.2 Inflation and Rising Costs

One of the most pressing economic challenges facing the United States under Biden's presidency is the rising inflation rate. Inflation refers to the general increase in prices of goods and services over time, eroding the purchasing power of individuals and businesses. In recent months, the country has experienced a significant uptick in inflation, with prices rising at the fastest pace in years.

Critics argue that Biden's expansive fiscal policies, coupled with supply chain disruptions and increased demand, have contributed to this surge in inflation. Rising costs of essential goods and services, such as housing, fuel, and groceries, have put a strain on American households and businesses. Small businesses, in particular, have been hit hard by the rising costs of raw materials and labor, making it increasingly challenging for them to operate and thrive.

8.3.3 Job Market and Employment

Another crucial aspect of the economic impact of Biden's political career is the state of the job market and employment. While the COVID-19 pandemic undoubtedly had a significant impact on the job market, Biden's policies and decisions have also played a role in shaping the employment landscape.

Supporters of Biden argue that his administration has made significant strides in job creation, pointing to the millions of jobs added since he took office. They highlight initiatives such as the infrastructure plan, which aims to create new employment opportunities in sectors like clean energy and transportation. However, critics argue that the job market recovery has been uneven, with certain industries and regions still struggling to regain pre-pandemic levels of employment.

Furthermore, concerns have been raised about the quality of jobs being created. Many of the new jobs are in low-wage sectors, and wage growth has not kept pace with the rising cost of living. This has led to a growing sense of economic insecurity among American workers, with many feeling left behind by the recovery.

8.3.4 Trade and Global Economic Relations

Biden's approach to trade and global economic relations has also had implications for the American economy. His administration has taken a more protectionist stance, emphasizing the need to prioritize American workers and industries. This has included renegotiating trade agreements, such as the United States-Mexico-Canada Agreement (USMCA), and imposing tariffs on certain goods.

While the intention behind these policies may be to protect American jobs and industries, critics argue that they can have unintended consequences. Trade restrictions and tariffs can lead to retaliatory measures from other countries, potentially harming American exporters and increasing costs for consumers. Additionally, a more protectionist approach may hinder economic growth and innovation by limiting access to global markets and disrupting supply chains.

8.3.5 Long-Term Implications and Future Challenges

The economic impact of Joseph Biden's political career is not limited to the present moment but will have long-term implications for the future of America. The decisions made today will shape the economic landscape for years to come, and it is essential to consider the potential challenges that lie ahead.

One of the key challenges facing the American economy is the national debt. The significant increase in government spending under Biden's leadership has contributed to a growing national debt, which now stands at unprecedented levels. This debt burden has the potential to limit future economic growth, increase interest payments, and constrain the government's ability to respond to future crises.

Another challenge is the need to address structural issues within the economy, such as income inequality and workforce development. While Biden has proposed various initiatives to tackle these issues, their effectiveness and long-term impact remain to be seen.

In conclusion, the economic impact of Joseph Biden's political career is a complex and multifaceted issue. His policies and decisions have had both positive and negative consequences for the American economy. While some argue that his actions have stimulated growth and addressed pressing challenges, others express concerns about the long-term implications of excessive government spending, rising inflation, and the national debt. As America moves forward, it will be crucial to assess and address these economic challenges to ensure a prosperous future for the nation.

8.4 Social and Cultural Divisions

Throughout Joseph Biden's political career, there have been numerous instances where his actions and policies have contributed to the deepening social and cultural divisions within the United States. From his time as a county council member to his current presidency, Biden's decisions have often prioritized partisan interests over the unity and well-being of the American people.

8.4.1 Identity Politics and Polarization

One of the key factors contributing to social and cultural divisions under Biden's leadership is the pervasive use of identity politics. Rather than focusing on policies that benefit all Americans, Biden has frequently resorted to appealing to specific identity groups, further polarizing the nation. This approach has only served to deepen existing divisions and create an "us versus them" mentality among different demographic groups.

8.4.2 Cancel Culture and Freedom of Speech

Another concerning aspect of Biden's presidency is the rise of cancel culture and the erosion of freedom of speech. Under the guise of promoting inclusivity and combating hate speech, there has been a growing trend of silencing dissenting voices and stifling open dialogue. This has created an environment where individuals fear expressing their opinions, leading to a chilling effect on free speech and a further fragmentation of society.

8.4.3 Racial Tensions and Identity Politics

Biden's handling of racial tensions has also contributed to social divisions. While he campaigned on promises of unity and healing, his actions have often exacerbated racial tensions rather than alleviating them. By embracing divisive rhetoric and policies that prioritize certain racial groups over others, Biden has deepened the divide between Americans of different races and ethnicities.

8.4.4 Cultural Values and Traditional Institutions

Biden's disregard for traditional cultural values and institutions has also played a role in widening social divisions. His administration has shown a lack of respect for religious freedoms and has taken steps to undermine the sanctity of life and traditional family structures. These actions have alienated a significant portion of the population who hold strong beliefs in these values, further fueling social and cultural divisions.

8.4.5 Urban-Rural Divide

The urban-rural divide has been a long-standing issue in American society, and Biden's policies have only exacerbated this divide. His focus on urban areas and neglect of rural communities has left many feeling neglected and marginalized. This divide has led to a sense of resentment and alienation among rural Americans, further deepening social divisions.

8.4.6 Education and Ideological Indoctrination

The education system plays a crucial role in shaping the values and beliefs of future generations. Unfortunately, under Biden's leadership, there has been a growing concern about ideological indoctrination in schools. The promotion of critical race theory and other divisive ideologies has led to increased polarization among students and their families. This ideological divide further contributes to the social and cultural divisions within the country.

8.4.7 Media Bias and Manipulation

The media's role in exacerbating social and cultural divisions cannot be overlooked. There is a clear bias in the mainstream media, with many outlets favoring Biden and his policies. This biased reporting has led to a lack of balanced and objective information, further polarizing the American public.

The manipulation of information and selective reporting have created echo chambers, where individuals are only exposed to viewpoints that align with their own, reinforcing existing divisions.

8.4.8 Lack of National Unity

Perhaps the most significant consequence of Biden's social and cultural divisions is the erosion of national unity. The United States has always prided itself on being a diverse nation with a shared sense of purpose and identity. However, under Biden's leadership, this unity has been eroded, and the country has become increasingly fragmented along ideological lines. This lack of national unity hinders progress and makes it difficult to address the pressing challenges facing the nation.

In conclusion, Joseph Biden's political career has been marked by a series of decisions and policies that have deepened social and cultural divisions within the United States. From the use of identity politics to the erosion of freedom of speech and the neglect of rural communities, Biden's actions have contributed to a fractured society. It is crucial for the American people to recognize these divisions and work towards healing and unity to ensure a brighter future for the nation.

9 Border Crises

9.1 Border Policies and Crisis

The border policies implemented by the Biden administration have led to a severe crisis at the United States-Mexico border. The consequences of these policies have been far-reaching, impacting both humanitarian concerns and national security.

Since taking office, President Biden has rolled back several immigration policies put in place by the previous administration. These policy changes, coupled with a more lenient approach to border enforcement, have created a magnet effect, drawing a significant influx of migrants to the southern border. The number of individuals attempting to cross the border illegally has reached alarming levels, overwhelming border patrol agents and immigration facilities.

One of the key factors contributing to the border crisis is the suspension of the "Remain in Mexico" policy, also known as the Migrant Protection Protocols (MPP). Under this policy, individuals seeking asylum in the United States were required to wait in Mexico until their cases were processed. This policy acted as a deterrent for illegal border crossings and helped manage the flow of migrants. However, the Biden administration's decision to end MPP has resulted in a surge of asylum seekers at the border, straining resources and creating a backlog in the immigration system.

Additionally, the Biden administration has implemented a more relaxed approach to interior enforcement, focusing on prioritizing the deportation of individuals with serious criminal records. This shift in policy has created an environment of lax enforcement, leading to an increase in illegal border crossings. Migrants, including families and unaccompanied minors, have taken advantage of this situation, hoping to gain entry into the United States.

The humanitarian concerns arising from the border crisis cannot be ignored. The surge in illegal border crossings has resulted in overcrowded detention facilities, where migrants, including children, are held in substandard conditions. The lack of adequate resources and infrastructure has put a strain on the ability to provide proper care and support for these individuals. The situation has raised questions about the administration's ability to handle the influx of migrants and ensure their well-being.

Furthermore, the border crisis has significant national security implications. The lack of effective border control measures allows for the potential entry of individuals with criminal backgrounds or ties to terrorist organizations. The overwhelmed border patrol agents are unable to thoroughly vet every individual crossing the border, creating a potential security risk for the United States. This poses a threat to the safety and well-being of American citizens.

The public response to the border crisis has been mixed. Supporters of the Biden administration argue that the policies are more compassionate and humane, emphasizing the need to provide refuge for those fleeing violence and persecution. They believe that the crisis is a result of long-standing systemic issues that require comprehensive immigration reform.

However, critics argue that the Biden administration's border policies have created an unmanageable situation, compromising both national security and the integrity of the immigration system. They believe that the lack of enforcement and clear messaging from the administration has incentivized illegal immigration and undermined the rule of law.

The House Committee's investigations have shed light on the role of Biden's family and their involvement with shell corporations. These revelations have raised concerns about potential conflicts of interest and the influence of foreign entities on the Biden administration's decision-making processes. The findings have further fueled the perception of corruption and nepotism within the Biden political career.

The evidence uncovered by the House Committee has added another layer of complexity to the already contentious issue of border policies. It has raised questions about the motivations behind certain policy decisions and the potential impact on national security. The public's perception of these revelations and their response to the crisis will undoubtedly shape the future of the Biden presidency.

In conclusion, the border policies implemented by the Biden administration have resulted in a severe crisis at the United States-Mexico border. The humanitarian concerns and national security implications cannot be ignored. The House Committee's findings regarding Biden's family and shell corporations have added to the complexity of the issue, raising questions about potential conflicts of interest and the influence of foreign entities. The public's response to the crisis and the evidence uncovered will play a crucial role in shaping the future of the Biden presidency.

9.2 Humanitarian Concerns

As we delve deeper into the political career of Joseph Biden, it becomes evident that his actions and policies have not only had detrimental effects on the United States but have also raised serious humanitarian concerns. Throughout his tenure as Vice President and now as President, Biden's approach to immigration and border security has resulted in a humanitarian crisis that cannot be ignored.

9.2.1 The Humanitarian Crisis at the Border

One of the most pressing issues that has emerged during Biden's presidency is the border crisis. Since taking office, Biden has implemented policies that have effectively weakened border security and created an environment that encourages illegal immigration. The consequences of these policies have been dire, with a significant increase in the number of individuals attempting to cross the border illegally.

The overcrowded detention facilities and the overwhelming number of migrants seeking entry into the United States have created a humanitarian crisis. The conditions in these facilities have been described as deplorable, with reports of overcrowding, unsanitary conditions, and a lack of basic necessities. The sheer volume of individuals crossing the border has stretched the resources of border patrol agents and overwhelmed the capacity of these facilities.

9.2.2 Human Trafficking and Exploitation

The lax approach to border security under the Biden administration has also led to an increase in human trafficking and exploitation. Criminal organizations and human smugglers have taken advantage of the situation, exploiting vulnerable individuals who are desperate to seek a better life in the United States. These individuals often fall victim to human trafficking networks, enduring unimaginable hardships and abuse along their journey.

The Biden administration's failure to effectively address this issue has allowed these criminal networks to flourish, putting countless lives at risk. The lack of comprehensive border security measures has made it easier for these criminal organizations to operate, further exacerbating the humanitarian crisis at the border.

9.2.3 Impact on Vulnerable Populations

The consequences of Biden's immigration policies extend beyond the immediate border crisis. The influx of undocumented immigrants has put a strain on social services and resources, affecting vulnerable populations within the United States. Limited resources that were meant to support American citizens and legal residents are now being diverted to accommodate the needs of undocumented immigrants.

This diversion of resources has had a detrimental impact on communities that were already struggling. The strain on healthcare, education, and social welfare systems has left many American citizens and legal residents without the support they need. This disregard for the well-being of vulnerable populations within the United States is a clear betrayal of Biden's duty as President.

9.2.4 Lack of Solutions and Accountability

Despite the severity of the humanitarian crisis at the border, the Biden administration has failed to provide effective solutions or take accountability for their actions. Instead of implementing policies that prioritize border security and the well-being of both American citizens and undocumented immigrants, the administration has focused on reversing the previous administration's policies without considering the consequences.

The lack of a comprehensive immigration plan and the failure to address the root causes of illegal immigration have only perpetuated the crisis. The Biden administration's unwillingness to acknowledge the failures of their policies and their refusal to work towards finding viable solutions have further deepened the humanitarian concerns at the border.

9.2.5 International Implications

The humanitarian crisis at the border also has significant international implications. The lack of control over the border not only undermines the security and sovereignty of the United States but also sends a message to the international community that the United States is unable to effectively manage its borders.

This perception weakens America's standing on the global stage and undermines its ability to address other pressing international issues. It also sets a dangerous precedent, as it encourages individuals from around the world to attempt illegal entry into the United States, further exacerbating the humanitarian crisis.

In conclusion, the humanitarian concerns arising from Biden's approach to immigration and border security cannot be ignored. The border crisis, human trafficking, exploitation, and the strain on resources have created a dire situation that demands immediate attention and effective solutions. The lack of accountability and the failure to address the root causes of the crisis only further highlight the betrayal of Biden's political career and the detrimental impact it has had on both the United States and vulnerable populations within its borders.

9.3 National Security Implications

National security is a critical aspect of any country's governance, ensuring the safety and well-being of its citizens. In the case of Joseph Biden's political career, there have been significant concerns regarding national security implications. From his time as Vice President to his current presidency, Biden's decisions and policies have raised questions about the safety and security of the United States.

9.3.1 Weakening Border Security

One of the most pressing national security concerns during Biden's presidency has been the border crisis and the subsequent weakening of border security. Since taking office, Biden has implemented policies that have led to a surge in illegal immigration, overwhelming border patrol agents and creating a humanitarian crisis at the southern border.

By reversing many of the previous administration's immigration policies, such as the "Remain in Mexico" policy and tightening asylum rules, Biden's administration has inadvertently sent a message that the United States has lax immigration enforcement. This has attracted a significant number of migrants, including individuals with criminal backgrounds and potential national security threats.

The lack of proper vetting and screening processes for those entering the country illegally raises serious concerns about potential terrorists or individuals with malicious intent slipping through the cracks. This poses a direct threat to national security, as it becomes increasingly challenging to identify and apprehend individuals who may pose a risk to the safety of American citizens.

9.3.2 Border Control and Drug Trafficking

The weakening of border security also has implications for drug trafficking and organized crime. With the surge in illegal border crossings, criminal organizations have found new opportunities to smuggle drugs, weapons, and contraband into the United States. This not only fuels the ongoing drug epidemic but also poses a significant threat to national security.

The influx of drugs, such as fentanyl and other opioids, has devastating consequences for American communities. The Biden administration's failure to effectively address this issue and secure the border has allowed drug cartels to exploit the situation, leading to an increase in drug-related violence and crime.

Furthermore, the porous border has created a gateway for human trafficking, endangering the lives of vulnerable individuals, including women and children. This not only violates human rights but also poses a national security risk, as criminal networks involved in human trafficking often have connections to other illicit activities, including terrorism.

9.3.3 Cybersecurity Vulnerabilities

In an increasingly digital world, cybersecurity has become a paramount concern for national security. The Biden administration's approach to cybersecurity has raised concerns about the country's ability to protect critical infrastructure and sensitive information from cyber threats.

Recent cyberattacks on major U.S. companies and government agencies, such as the Colonial Pipeline and SolarWinds incidents, have highlighted the vulnerabilities in the nation's cybersecurity defenses. These attacks, often attributed to foreign adversaries, have the potential to disrupt essential services, compromise national security, and undermine public trust.

Biden's response to these cyber threats has been criticized for being reactive rather than proactive. The lack of a comprehensive cybersecurity strategy and failure to invest adequately in cybersecurity infrastructure leaves the United States vulnerable to future attacks. This not only puts national security at risk but also has economic and societal implications.

9.3.4 International Relations and Alliances

National security is closely tied to a country's relationships with other nations and its ability to form strong alliances. During his political career, Biden's decisions and actions have raised concerns about the United States' standing on the global stage and its ability to effectively address international security challenges.

Biden's approach to foreign policy has been characterized by a shift away from the principles of American exceptionalism and a more globalist agenda. This has led to strained relationships with traditional allies, such as Israel, and a perceived lack of commitment to defending shared values and interests.

Furthermore, Biden's decision to reenter international agreements, such as the Paris Climate Accord and the Iran Nuclear Deal, without securing significant concessions or addressing underlying concerns, has raised questions about the administration's commitment to protecting national security interests.

The weakening of alliances and strained international relationships can have far-reaching implications for national security. It reduces the United States' ability to effectively address global security challenges, respond to emerging threats, and protect its interests abroad.

9.3.5 Public Opinion and Response

The national security implications of Biden's political career have not gone unnoticed by the American public. As the consequences of his policies become more apparent, there has been a growing concern among citizens regarding the safety and security of the nation.

Public opinion polls have shown a decline in confidence in Biden's ability to handle national security issues effectively. Many Americans feel that his decisions and policies have weakened the country's position on the global stage and compromised its ability to protect its citizens from potential threats.

The response to these concerns has varied, with some advocating for a more robust approach to national security and border control, while others support Biden's more inclusive and globalist agenda. The debate surrounding national security implications remains a contentious issue, with both sides presenting valid arguments.

In conclusion, the national security implications of Joseph Biden's political career are significant and cannot be ignored. From the weakening of border security to cybersecurity vulnerabilities and strained international relationships, there are legitimate concerns about the safety and security of the United States. As the nation grapples with these challenges, it is crucial to assess and address the implications of Biden's decisions and policies to ensure the protection of American citizens and the preservation of national security.

9.4 Public Opinion and Response

Public opinion plays a crucial role in shaping the political landscape of any country. It is the collective voice of the people, reflecting their thoughts, beliefs, and sentiments towards their leaders and the policies they implement. In the case of Joseph Biden, his political career has been marred by controversy, corruption, and broken promises, leading to a significant impact on public opinion and response.

9.4.1 Initial Expectations and Disillusionment

When Joseph Biden first entered politics, many people had high hopes for him. They saw him as a fresh face, someone who could bring about positive change and address the pressing issues facing the nation. However, as time went on, these initial expectations began to fade, replaced by disillusionment and a growing sense of betrayal.

9.4.2 Broken Promises and False Hope

Throughout his political career, Biden made numerous promises to the American people. He pledged to tackle corruption, improve the economy, and restore America's standing in the world. However, time and again, these promises proved to be nothing more than empty rhetoric.

One of the most glaring examples of broken promises was Biden's handling of the border crisis. During his presidential campaign, he promised to address the issue and implement effective immigration policies. Yet, since taking office, the situation at the border has only worsened, with a surge in illegal crossings and a lack of meaningful action to address the root causes of the crisis.

9.4.3 Lack of Transparency and Accountability

Another factor that has contributed to public opinion turning against Biden is the lack of transparency and accountability in his administration. The revelations about his family's involvement in questionable business dealings and the existence of shell corporations have raised serious concerns about potential conflicts of interest and corruption.

The House Committee's findings have shed light on these issues, exposing a web of financial entanglements that raise questions about Biden's integrity and his ability to make decisions in the best interest of the American people. This lack of transparency and accountability has eroded public trust and further fueled the perception of a betrayal by the President.

9.4.4 Polarization and Divisions

The controversies surrounding Biden's political career have also contributed to the deepening polarization and divisions within the country. As public opinion becomes more divided, it becomes increasingly difficult to find common ground and work towards meaningful solutions to the challenges facing the nation.

The media's role in shaping public opinion cannot be overlooked. The biased reporting and selective coverage have further fueled the divisions, with different segments of the population receiving different narratives and interpretations of the same events. This has led to a fragmented understanding of the issues and a lack of consensus on the way forward.

9.4.5 Grassroots Movements and Activism

In response to the perceived betrayal by Biden, grassroots movements and activism have emerged across the country. These movements aim to hold the

President accountable for his actions, demand transparency, and push for policy changes that align with the interests of the American people.

These movements have gained traction through social media platforms, allowing like-minded individuals to connect, organize, and amplify their voices. They have become a powerful force in shaping public opinion and putting pressure on the administration to address the concerns of the people.

9.4.6 The Role of Public Opinion in Democracy

Public opinion serves as a vital check on the power of political leaders. It holds them accountable for their actions and decisions, ensuring that they remain responsive to the needs and aspirations of the people they serve. In the case of Joseph Biden, public opinion has played a significant role in highlighting the shortcomings of his political career and the impact of his policies on the nation.

As public opinion continues to evolve and shape the political landscape, it is essential for leaders to listen to the concerns of the people and take meaningful action to address them. Failure to do so can result in further erosion of trust and a deepening divide between the government and the governed.

In conclusion, public opinion and response to Joseph Biden's political career have been largely negative, driven by broken promises, lack of transparency, and perceived betrayal. The House Committee's findings regarding his family's involvement in questionable business dealings have further fueled public distrust. Grassroots movements and activism have emerged as a response to these concerns, highlighting the importance of public opinion in holding leaders accountable and shaping the future of the nation.

10 Inflation

10.1 Causes of Inflation

Inflation is a complex economic phenomenon that affects the purchasing power of a nation's currency. It occurs when there is a sustained increase in the general price level of goods and services over a period of time. In recent years, the United States has experienced a significant rise in inflation, which has had far-reaching consequences for the economy and the American people. In this section, we will explore the causes of inflation and how government spending and policies have contributed to this economic challenge.

10.1.1 Monetary Factors

One of the primary causes of inflation is an increase in the money supply. When the government or central bank prints more money or injects it into the economy through various channels, it can lead to an excess supply of money in circulation. This excess money chases the same amount of goods and services, driving up prices. The Federal Reserve, the central bank of the United States, plays a crucial role in managing the money supply and controlling inflation through its monetary policy decisions.

10.1.2 Government Spending and Deficit

Government spending can also contribute to inflation. When the government spends more money than it collects in revenue, it creates a budget deficit. To finance this deficit, the government may resort to borrowing or printing more money. Increased government spending without a corresponding increase in productivity or output can put upward pressure on prices. Additionally, when the government borrows money, it competes with private borrowers for available funds, leading to higher interest rates and increased costs for businesses and consumers.

10.1.3 Demand-Pull Inflation

Demand-pull inflation occurs when there is an increase in aggregate demand for goods and services that outpaces the economy's ability to supply them. This can happen due to factors such as increased consumer spending, government stimulus programs, or expansionary monetary policies. When demand exceeds supply, businesses may raise prices to capitalize on the increased demand, leading to inflationary pressures.

10.1.4 Cost-Push Inflation

Cost-push inflation occurs when there is an increase in production costs that is passed on to consumers in the form of higher prices. This can happen due to factors such as rising wages, increased raw material costs, or higher taxes and regulations imposed on businesses. When businesses face higher costs, they may raise prices to maintain their profit margins, contributing to inflation.

10.1.5 Global Factors

Global factors can also influence inflation in the United States. Changes in international commodity prices, exchange rates, or global supply chains can impact the cost of imported goods and raw materials. If the value of the U.S. dollar depreciates relative to other currencies, it can make imports more expensive, leading to higher prices for consumers. Additionally, geopolitical events or disruptions in global markets can create volatility and uncertainty, which can affect inflationary pressures.

10.1.6 Expectations and Psychology

Expectations and psychology play a significant role in shaping inflationary trends. If businesses and consumers anticipate higher future prices, they may adjust their behavior accordingly. Businesses may raise prices in anticipation of increased costs, and consumers may accelerate their spending to avoid paying higher prices later. These expectations can become self-fulfilling, leading to a cycle of rising prices and inflation.

10.1.7 Government Policies and Regulations

Government policies and regulations can have unintended consequences on inflation. Excessive regulations and bureaucratic red tape can increase production costs for businesses, leading to higher prices. Additionally, policies that distort market forces, such as price controls or subsidies, can disrupt supply and demand dynamics, contributing to inflationary pressures.

10.1.8 Impact on the Economy

The consequences of inflation can be far-reaching and detrimental to the economy. When prices rise, the purchasing power of individuals and households decreases, making it more challenging to afford goods and services. This can lead to a decline in consumer confidence and spending, which can negatively impact businesses and economic growth. Additionally, inflation erodes the value of savings and fixed-income investments, disproportionately affecting retirees and those on fixed incomes.

10.1.9 Public Perception and Consequences

The public's perception of inflation can have significant consequences. When individuals and businesses anticipate higher future prices, they may adjust their behavior by demanding higher wages or increasing prices, further fueling inflationary pressures. Additionally, inflation can erode trust in the government's ability to manage the economy and maintain price stability, leading to a loss of confidence in the overall economic system.

In conclusion, inflation is a complex economic phenomenon influenced by various factors, including monetary policies, government spending, demand and supply dynamics, global factors, expectations, and government regulations. Understanding the causes of inflation is crucial for policymakers to implement effective measures to mitigate its negative impacts on the economy and the well-being of the American people.

10.2 Government Spending and Policies

Government spending and policies play a crucial role in shaping the economic landscape of a nation. In the case of Joseph Biden's political career, his approach to government spending and policies has been a cause for concern. Throughout his tenure as a public servant, Biden has consistently advocated for policies that have had a detrimental impact on the economy and the American people.

10.2.1 Excessive Government Spending

One of the key issues surrounding Biden's government spending policies is the excessive amount of money being allocated to various programs and initiatives. Throughout his career, Biden has consistently supported bloated budgets and increased government intervention in the economy. This approach has led to a significant increase in the national debt and has put a strain on future generations who will be burdened with the task of repaying this debt.

Biden's support for massive spending bills, such as the American Rescue Plan and the Build Back Better Plan, has raised concerns about the long-term sustainability of these policies. While these plans may promise short-term relief and economic stimulus, they come at a high cost and have the potential to exacerbate inflation and weaken the overall economy.

10.2.2 Ineffective Policies

In addition to excessive spending, Biden's policies have also been criticized for their ineffectiveness. Despite promising to deliver economic growth and prosperity, many of Biden's policies have failed to achieve their intended outcomes. For example, his push for clean energy initiatives and the Green New Deal has resulted in job losses in industries such as coal and oil, without providing viable alternatives for those affected.

Furthermore, Biden's approach to taxation and regulation has hindered business growth and innovation. His proposed tax increases on corporations and high-income individuals have the potential to stifle economic growth and discourage investment. Additionally, his support for burdensome regulations has created barriers for small businesses and hindered their ability to thrive and create jobs.

10.2.3 Impact on the Economy

The consequences of Biden's government spending and policies are already being felt in the economy. One of the most significant concerns is the rising inflation rate. Inflation erodes the purchasing power of individuals and leads to higher prices for goods and services. The excessive government spending and loose monetary policies advocated by Biden have contributed to the current inflationary pressures.

Moreover, the increase in government debt resulting from Biden's spending policies has long-term implications for the economy. As the national debt continues to grow, it places a burden on future generations who will be responsible for paying off this debt. This can lead to higher taxes, reduced government services, and a less prosperous future for the American people.

10.2.4 Public Perception and Consequences

The impact of Biden's government spending and policies has not gone unnoticed by the American people. Many individuals are concerned about the long-term consequences of these policies and the potential harm they may cause to the economy. Rising inflation, job losses, and increased taxes are all factors that contribute to a growing sense of unease and dissatisfaction among the public.

Furthermore, the perception of wasteful government spending and ineffective policies has eroded trust in the government and its ability to effectively manage the economy. This lack of trust can have far-reaching consequences, including a decline in public confidence, reduced investment, and a slower economic recovery.

In conclusion, Joseph Biden's approach to government spending and policies has had a detrimental impact on the economy and the American people. His support for excessive spending, ineffective policies, and the resulting inflationary pressures have raised concerns about the long-term sustainability of his economic agenda. The consequences of these policies are already being felt, and the public's perception of wasteful spending and ineffective policies has further eroded trust in the government. It is essential to reassess these policies and prioritize responsible fiscal management to ensure a prosperous future for the United States.

10.3 Effects on the Economy

The economic policies implemented by Joseph Biden during his presidency have had significant effects on the economy of the United States. From the early days of his administration, it became evident that his approach to economic management would have far-reaching consequences. Unfortunately, these consequences have not been positive for the American people.

One of the most concerning effects of Biden's economic policies has been the rapid rise in inflation. Inflation refers to the general increase in prices of goods and services over time, resulting in a decrease in the purchasing power of money. Under Biden's watch, inflation has soared to levels not seen in decades. This has had a direct impact on the everyday lives of Americans, as the cost of essential goods and services has skyrocketed. From groceries to gasoline, Americans are feeling the pinch of higher prices, making it increasingly difficult to make ends meet.

The causes of this inflationary surge can be traced back to the government's excessive spending and policies. Biden's administration has pursued a massive expansion of government programs and initiatives, leading to a surge in government spending. This increased spending has been financed through borrowing and printing more money, which has flooded the economy with excess cash. As a result, the value of the dollar has decreased, leading to higher prices for goods and services.

Furthermore, Biden's policies have also had a detrimental effect on job creation and economic growth. His administration's focus on increasing regulations and implementing higher taxes on businesses has created a hostile environment for job creators. Small businesses, in particular, have been hit hard by these policies, struggling to stay afloat amidst the burdensome regulations and increased tax burdens. As a result, job growth has been sluggish, and many Americans continue to face unemployment or underemployment.

The effects of Biden's economic policies extend beyond inflation and job creation. The increased government intervention in the economy has stifled innovation and entrepreneurship. When the government becomes overly involved in dictating economic outcomes, it hampers the free market's ability to allocate resources efficiently. This leads to a less dynamic and innovative economy, hindering long-term economic growth and prosperity.

Moreover, the uncertainty surrounding Biden's economic policies has also had a negative impact on business investment and consumer confidence. Businesses thrive in an environment of stability and predictability, allowing them to plan for the future and make informed decisions. However, the constant changes and reversals in economic policies under the Biden administration have created an atmosphere of uncertainty. This has made businesses hesitant to invest and expand, leading to a slowdown in economic activity.

The effects of Biden's economic policies have not gone unnoticed by the American people. Public perception of the economy under his leadership has been largely negative. Many Americans feel the pinch of rising prices and stagnant wages, making it increasingly difficult to achieve financial security. The middle class, in particular, has been hit hard, as they bear the brunt of the economic burden.

Furthermore, the consequences of Biden's economic policies extend beyond the immediate impact on individuals and businesses. The long-term implications of excessive government spending and inflation are concerning. As the national debt continues to soar, future generations will be burdened with the responsibility of paying off this debt. This will limit their opportunities and hinder their ability to achieve economic prosperity.

In conclusion, the effects of Joseph Biden's economic policies on the economy have been detrimental. The rapid rise in inflation, sluggish job growth, stifled innovation, and decreased consumer confidence are all consequences of his approach to economic management. The American people are feeling the impact of these policies in their everyday lives, as the cost of living continues to rise. It is crucial to reassess these policies and implement measures that promote economic growth, job creation, and stability. Only then can the United States rebuild its economy and secure a prosperous future for its citizens.

10.4 Public Perception and Consequences

Public perception plays a crucial role in shaping the political landscape and determining the consequences of a politician's actions. In the case of Joseph Biden, his political career has been marred by controversies, scandals, and a series of broken promises. As the public becomes increasingly aware of the truth behind his actions, the consequences of his decisions are becoming more apparent.

10.4.1 The Erosion of Trust

One of the most significant consequences of Joseph Biden's political career is the erosion of trust between the American people and their government. Throughout his time in office, Biden has made numerous promises to the public, only to break them once in power. From his early years in the New Castle County Council to his presidency, Biden has consistently failed to deliver on his commitments, leaving the public disillusioned and skeptical of his intentions.

10.4.2 Loss of Confidence in Leadership

The lack of transparency and accountability in Biden's political career has led to a loss of confidence in his leadership. The American people expect their leaders to act with integrity and honesty, but Biden's track record suggests otherwise. The revelations of corruption, nepotism, and the use of shell corporations by his family have further eroded public trust in his ability to lead effectively.

10.4.3 Economic Consequences

Biden's policies and actions have had significant economic consequences for the American people. One of the most pressing issues is the alarming rise in inflation. The unchecked government spending and policies implemented by the Biden administration have contributed to the devaluation of the dollar and increased prices for everyday goods and services. As a result, American families are struggling to make ends meet, and businesses are facing financial hardships.

10.4.4 Burden on Future Generations

The consequences of Biden's political career extend beyond the present moment and will burden future generations. The excessive government spending and mounting national debt will have long-term implications for the economy and the financial stability of the country. The choices made by Biden and his administration will ultimately be inherited by future generations, leaving them with the responsibility of addressing the economic challenges created by his policies.

10.4.5 Polarization and Divisions

Biden's presidency has also contributed to the deepening polarization and divisions within American society. His divisive rhetoric and policies have further fueled the already existing social and cultural divisions. The lack of unity and the inability to bridge the gap between different ideological perspectives have hindered progress and hindered the ability to address pressing issues facing the nation.

10.4.6 International Standing

The consequences of Biden's political career extend beyond domestic affairs and have had a significant impact on America's standing in the international community. His foreign policy decisions, such as the hasty withdrawal from Afghanistan, have raised concerns about America's reliability as a global leader. The strained relationships with key allies and the failure to effectively address international challenges have weakened America's position on the world stage.

10.4.7 Backlash and Resistance

As the truth about Biden's political career continues to emerge, there has been a growing backlash and resistance from the American people. Citizens who once supported him are now questioning his integrity and ability to lead. Grassroots movements and organizations have formed to hold him accountable for his actions and to advocate for a more transparent and accountable government.

10.4.8 Rebuilding Trust and Moving Forward

Rebuilding trust and moving forward will require a comprehensive reassessment of the political system and a commitment to transparency and accountability. The American people deserve leaders who prioritize their interests and uphold the values of honesty and integrity. It is essential to learn from the mistakes of the past and work towards a future where public officials are held accountable for their actions and where the trust of the people is restored.

In conclusion, the public perception of Joseph Biden's political career has been shaped by broken promises, corruption, and scandals. The consequences of his actions are evident in the erosion of trust, loss of confidence in leadership, economic challenges, polarization, and divisions within society, weakened international standing, and a growing backlash from the American people. Moving forward, it is crucial to rebuild trust, hold leaders accountable, and work towards a more transparent and accountable government for the betterment of the nation and its future generations.

11 Undermining the United States

11.1 Foreign Policy Decisions

Foreign policy decisions play a crucial role in shaping a nation's standing in the global arena. It is through these decisions that leaders establish relationships with other countries, protect national interests, and promote peace and stability. In the case of Joseph Biden, his foreign policy decisions have been a subject of scrutiny and concern.

Throughout his political career, Biden has made several foreign policy decisions that have raised eyebrows and sparked debates. Critics argue that these decisions have undermined the United States' position on the world stage and have had far-reaching implications for the country's national interests.

One of the key foreign policy decisions made by Biden was the withdrawal of U.S. troops from Afghanistan. While the idea of ending America's longest war was widely supported, the execution of the withdrawal was heavily criticized. The abrupt and chaotic manner in which the withdrawal took place resulted in the Taliban's rapid takeover of the country and the collapse of the Afghan government. This decision not only jeopardized the lives of Afghan citizens who had supported the U.S., but it also raised concerns about the resurgence of terrorism in the region.

Another controversial foreign policy decision made by Biden was the re-entry of the United States into the Paris Agreement on climate change. While the agreement itself aims to address the global challenge of climate change, critics argue that the terms of the agreement disproportionately burden the United States and hinder its economic growth. By rejoining the agreement without negotiating better terms for the country, Biden has been accused of prioritizing global interests over national interests.

Biden's approach to China has also been a subject of scrutiny. While he has acknowledged the need to address China's unfair trade practices and human rights abuses, critics argue that his administration has not taken strong enough actions to hold China accountable. The lack of a clear and assertive strategy towards China has raised concerns about the United States' ability to protect its economic and national security interests in the face of an increasingly assertive China.

Furthermore, Biden's decision to lift sanctions on Iran and re-enter the Joint Comprehensive Plan of Action (JCPOA), commonly known as the Iran nuclear deal, has drawn criticism from those who believe that the deal does not do enough to prevent Iran from obtaining nuclear weapons. Critics argue that by re-entering the deal without securing stronger provisions, Biden has compromised the United States' national security and the security of its allies in the Middle East.

In addition to these specific foreign policy decisions, Biden's overall approach to international relations has been characterized by a shift towards multilateralism and a departure from the "America First" policy of his predecessor. While some argue that this approach strengthens alliances and promotes global cooperation, others believe that it undermines the United States' ability to prioritize its own national interests.

The implications of Biden's foreign policy decisions for America's standing in the world are significant. Critics argue that his decisions have weakened the United States' position as a global leader and have eroded trust and confidence in American leadership. They argue that by prioritizing global interests over national interests, Biden has undermined the United States' ability to protect its economic and national security.

In conclusion, Joseph Biden's foreign policy decisions have been a subject of controversy and concern. Critics argue that these decisions have undermined the United States' position on the world stage and have had far-reaching implications for the country's national interests. Whether it is the withdrawal from Afghanistan, re-entry into the Paris Agreement, or the approach towards China and Iran, Biden's foreign policy decisions have raised questions about his ability to protect and promote America's interests in an increasingly complex and competitive global landscape.

11.2 Alliances and Relationships

Throughout his political career, Joseph Biden has claimed to be a champion of diplomacy and international cooperation. He has often emphasized the importance of alliances and relationships in shaping America's foreign policy. However, a closer examination of his actions reveals a pattern of undermining these alliances and damaging relationships with key global partners.

11.2.1 Weakening Traditional Alliances

One of the most concerning aspects of Biden's approach to international relations is his disregard for longstanding alliances. Traditional allies such as Israel, the United Kingdom, and Saudi Arabia have all experienced strained relationships under his leadership. Biden's decision to re-enter the Iran nuclear deal without consulting these allies has not only undermined their trust but also jeopardized regional stability.

Furthermore, his administration's handling of the withdrawal from Afghanistan has left NATO allies feeling abandoned and betrayed. The abrupt and chaotic manner in which the withdrawal was executed not only endangered the lives of Afghan allies but also damaged America's reputation as a reliable partner. This has raised serious doubts among NATO members about the United States' commitment to collective defense.

11.2.2 Embracing Adversaries

While Biden has shown a willingness to distance himself from traditional allies, he has displayed a concerning level of leniency towards adversaries. His administration's approach to China, for example, has been marked by a lack of firmness and a failure to hold the Chinese government accountable for its human rights abuses and unfair trade practices. This has emboldened China and weakened America's position on the global stage.

Similarly, Biden's decision to lift sanctions on Russia's Nord Stream 2 pipeline project, despite bipartisan opposition, has raised questions about his commitment to countering Russian aggression. This move not only undermines the energy security of Ukraine and Eastern European countries but also sends a message that the United States is willing to compromise its principles for the sake of appeasement.

11.2.3 Neglecting Regional Partnerships

In addition to weakening traditional alliances and embracing adversaries, Biden has also neglected regional partnerships that are crucial for maintaining stability in key areas of the world. For instance, his administration's lack of engagement with Latin American countries has allowed China to expand its influence in the region unchecked. This has significant implications for America's national security and economic interests.

Furthermore, Biden's decision to re-enter the Paris Agreement without addressing the concerns of countries like India and Brazil has strained relationships with these important regional players. By prioritizing climate change over other pressing issues, Biden has failed to recognize the need for a balanced approach that takes into account the unique challenges faced by different countries.

11.2.4 Undermining America's Standing

The consequences of Biden's approach to alliances and relationships are far-reaching and have serious implications for America's standing in the world. By weakening traditional alliances, embracing adversaries, and neglecting regional partnerships, he has eroded trust and damaged America's reputation as a reliable and principled global leader.

This erosion of trust has real-world consequences. It weakens America's ability to rally international support for important causes, such as countering Chinese aggression or addressing global challenges like climate change. It also undermines the effectiveness of international institutions and diminishes America's influence in shaping the rules-based international order.

In conclusion, Joseph Biden's approach to alliances and relationships has been marked by a disregard for traditional allies, a leniency towards adversaries, and a neglect of regional partnerships. This has resulted in a weakened America, both in terms of its reputation and its ability to effectively address global challenges. The implications of these actions are significant and will have lasting consequences for America's standing in the world.

11.3 National Interests vs. Global Agenda

As Joseph Biden's political career progressed, it became increasingly evident that his priorities lay more with a global agenda rather than the national interests of the United States. Throughout his time in various political positions, Biden consistently made decisions and pursued policies that seemed to prioritize international relationships and global initiatives over the well-being and prosperity of his own country.

11.3.1 Neglecting National Interests

One of the key aspects of Biden's approach to international relations was his tendency to neglect the national interests of the United States. Instead of prioritizing the economic, security, and social concerns of his own country, Biden often seemed more focused on appeasing international partners and pursuing a globalist agenda.

During his tenure as Vice President, Biden played a significant role in the Obama administration's foreign policy decisions. However, many of these decisions seemed to prioritize global interests over those of the United States. For example, the administration's approach to trade agreements, such as the Trans-Pacific Partnership (TPP), raised concerns about the potential negative impact on American industries and jobs.

11.3.2 Globalist Agenda

Biden's globalist agenda was evident in his approach to international alliances and relationships. While alliances and partnerships can be beneficial for a country, it is crucial to strike a balance that protects national interests and sovereignty. However, Biden's actions often seemed to prioritize maintaining relationships and appeasing international partners, even at the expense of American interests.

One example of this was Biden's approach to the Iran nuclear deal. Despite concerns about the deal's effectiveness in preventing Iran from obtaining nuclear weapons, Biden supported the agreement, seemingly more concerned with maintaining international relationships than with protecting the security interests of the United States and its allies in the Middle East.

11.3.3 Neglecting America's Standing

Biden's prioritization of a global agenda over national interests had significant implications for America's standing in the world. By neglecting the needs and concerns of his own country, Biden inadvertently weakened America's position on the global stage.

Under Biden's leadership, the United States faced criticism for its perceived lack of leadership and assertiveness in international affairs. This was particularly evident in the realm of foreign policy, where Biden's decisions and actions often seemed to prioritize maintaining relationships and avoiding confrontation, even when it came at the expense of American interests.

Furthermore, Biden's neglect of America's standing was also reflected in his approach to issues such as immigration and border security. By adopting lenient policies and failing to address the border crisis effectively, Biden sent a message that the United States was more concerned with accommodating the needs of migrants than with protecting its own borders and citizens.

11.3.4 Implications for America's Standing

The implications of Biden's prioritization of a global agenda over national interests are far-reaching and have the potential to impact America's standing in the world for years to come. By neglecting the needs and concerns of his own country, Biden has weakened America's position as a global leader and undermined its ability to effectively address pressing domestic issues.

Furthermore, Biden's approach to international relations has raised concerns about the long-term consequences for American sovereignty and independence. By prioritizing global initiatives and partnerships, Biden has opened the door for potential encroachments on American decision-making and policy autonomy.

In conclusion, Joseph Biden's political career has been marked by a prioritization of a global agenda over the national interests of the United States. From neglecting national interests to pursuing a globalist agenda, Biden's actions and decisions have had significant implications for America's standing in the world. As the evidence uncovered by the House Committee reveals, his family's involvement in shell corporations only adds to the concerns about his commitment to serving the American people. It is crucial for the future of the nation to assess and learn from the consequences of this betrayal, and to work towards rebuilding America's strength and prosperity.

11.4 Implications for America's Standing

The political career of Joseph Biden has had far-reaching implications for America's standing on the global stage. From his time as Vice President to his current role as President, Biden's decisions and actions have had a significant impact on the perception of the United States both domestically and internationally. In this section, we will explore the implications of Biden's policies and actions on America's standing in the world.

11.4.1 Weakening Alliances and Relationships

One of the key implications of Biden's foreign policy decisions has been the weakening of alliances and relationships with traditional allies. Throughout his presidency, Biden has taken actions that have strained relationships with countries such as Israel, Saudi Arabia, and Poland. These actions have not only undermined trust and cooperation but have also left a void that could be filled by other global powers, potentially diminishing America's influence and standing.

11.4.2 Undermining National Interests for a Global Agenda

Another implication of Biden's approach to international relations is the prioritization of a global agenda over national interests. Biden has shown a willingness to make concessions and compromises that may not align with the best interests of the United States. This approach has raised concerns among many Americans who believe that the President should prioritize the well-being and security of the nation above all else.

11.4.3 Damage to America's Reputation

Biden's actions and policies have also had a negative impact on America's reputation around the world. The perception of the United States as a strong and reliable global leader has been eroded by decisions such as the withdrawal from Afghanistan, which was widely criticized for its chaotic execution and the abandonment of Afghan allies. These actions have raised questions about America's commitment to its allies and its ability to effectively navigate international challenges.

11.4.4 Weakening of National Security

The implications of Biden's foreign policy decisions extend beyond reputation damage. There are concerns that his approach has weakened America's national security. For example, the decision to re-enter the Iran nuclear deal without addressing key concerns has raised fears about the potential for a nuclear-armed Iran. Additionally, the withdrawal of troops from Afghanistan without a clear plan has created a power vacuum that could be exploited by terrorist organizations, posing a direct threat to American national security.

11.4.5 Economic Consequences

Biden's policies and decisions have also had economic implications for the United States. The massive government spending and inflationary measures implemented under his administration have raised concerns about the long-term stability of the economy. The increasing national debt and rising inflation rates have the potential to undermine America's economic standing and weaken its position as a global economic powerhouse.

11.4.6 Diminished Influence on the World Stage

Perhaps one of the most significant implications of Biden's political career is the diminished influence of the United States on the world stage. The lack of a clear and coherent foreign policy strategy, coupled with questionable decision-making, has resulted in a loss of credibility and influence for the United States. This has allowed other global powers, such as China and Russia, to fill the void and exert greater influence over international affairs.

11.4.7 Erosion of Trust and Confidence

The implications of Biden's political career extend beyond policy decisions and economic consequences. There has been a noticeable erosion of trust and confidence in the United States under his leadership. The mishandling of various crises, such as the border crisis and the withdrawal from Afghanistan, has raised doubts about the competence and effectiveness of the Biden administration. This erosion of trust can have long-lasting implications for America's standing in the world and its ability to rally international support when needed.

In conclusion, Joseph Biden's political career has had significant implications for America's standing in the world. From weakening alliances and relationships to prioritizing a global agenda over national interests, his decisions and actions have had far-reaching consequences. The damage to America's reputation, the potential threats to national security, and the economic consequences all contribute to a diminished influence on the world stage. Furthermore, the erosion of trust and confidence in the United States under his leadership has further undermined America's standing. These implications highlight the need for a reassessment of Biden's political career and its impact on the future of America.

12 The Future of America

12.1 Assessing Biden's Political Career

Joseph Biden's political career has been marked by a series of controversies, scandals, and broken promises. From his early years in the New Castle County Council to his tenure as Vice President and eventually President of the United States, Biden's actions have had far-reaching consequences for the American people and the nation as a whole.

12.1.1 False Promises and Betrayal

Throughout his political career, Biden has made numerous promises to the American people, only to betray them time and time again. From his early days in the New Castle County Council, Biden showcased a pattern of making grandiose promises without delivering on them. Whether it was his pledge to tackle corruption or improve the lives of his constituents, Biden's actions rarely matched his words.

12.1.2 Corruption and Scandals

Biden's political career has been marred by allegations of corruption and scandals. From his involvement in the Ukraine scandal to his questionable business dealings with foreign entities, Biden's actions have raised serious ethical concerns. The recent revelations about his family's involvement in shell corporations and potential conflicts of interest have only further tarnished his reputation.

12.1.3 Impact on New Castle County

During his time in the New Castle County Council, Biden's actions had a significant impact on the local community. Despite his promises to improve the lives of his constituents, the reality was quite different. The county faced numerous challenges, including rising crime rates, economic stagnation, and a lack of transparency in government. Biden's tenure in the council did little to address these issues, leaving the residents of New Castle County disillusioned and betrayed.

12.1.4 Legislative Record

As a Senator, Biden's legislative record is a mixed bag. While he touted himself as a champion of the working class and a defender of civil rights, his actual accomplishments were limited. Biden's support for the controversial 1994 crime bill, which disproportionately affected minority communities, is a stain on his record. Additionally, his role in crafting the 2005 bankruptcy bill, which favored credit card companies over struggling individuals, further highlights his questionable priorities.

12.1.5 Controversial Votes

Throughout his Senate career, Biden made several controversial votes that have had lasting consequences. From his support for the Iraq War to his opposition to school busing, Biden's decisions often seemed out of touch with the needs and desires of the American people. These votes not only showcased a lack of judgment but also raised questions about his ability to make sound decisions on behalf of the nation.

12.1.6 Influence and Power

As Vice President, Biden wielded significant influence and power within the Obama administration. However, his tenure was marked by a lack of substantial accomplishments. Despite being tasked with overseeing the economic recovery and leading efforts to combat climate change, Biden's impact was minimal. His inability to effectively navigate the political landscape and deliver on his promises further highlights his shortcomings as a leader.

12.1.7 Legacy as Vice President

Biden's legacy as Vice President is one of missed opportunities and unfulfilled promises. Despite his claims of being a champion for the middle class, the economic recovery under the Obama administration was lackluster at best. Additionally, Biden's foreign policy decisions, such as the handling of the Syrian civil war and the rise of ISIS, have had long-lasting negative consequences. His inability to effectively address these challenges raises serious doubts about his ability to lead the nation.

12.1.8 Lessons from the Betrayal

The betrayal of the American people by Joseph Biden serves as a stark reminder of the importance of holding politicians accountable. It highlights the need for transparency, integrity, and a commitment to the well-being of the nation. The lessons learned from Biden's political career should serve as a wake-up call for the American people to demand better from their elected officials and to carefully scrutinize the promises made by those seeking public office.

12.1.9 Rebuilding America

Moving forward, it is crucial to focus on rebuilding America and restoring trust in the political system. This requires a commitment to ethical leadership, a dedication to the principles of democracy, and a focus on the needs of the American people. By learning from the mistakes of the past and holding our leaders accountable, we can work towards a brighter future for our nation.

12.1.10 Conclusion

Joseph Biden's political career has been marked by a series of betrayals, broken promises, and questionable actions. From his early years in the New Castle County Council to his time as Vice President and eventually President, Biden's actions have had far-reaching consequences for the American people.

It is essential to assess his political career critically and learn from the mistakes made to ensure a better future for our nation.

12.2 Lessons from the Betrayal

The political career of Joseph Biden has been marked by a series of betrayals and broken promises. From his early years in the New Castle County Council to his time as Vice President and eventually President of the United States, Biden's actions have consistently undermined the trust of the American people. As we reflect on the betrayal that has unfolded, there are several important lessons that we can learn.

12.2.1 The Danger of False Promises

One of the most significant lessons from Biden's betrayal is the danger of false promises. Throughout his career, Biden has made grandiose pledges to the American people, only to fall short on delivering them. Whether it was his promises of transparency and accountability or his commitment to economic prosperity, Biden's words have proven to be empty rhetoric. This serves as a reminder that we must be cautious and skeptical of politicians who make lofty promises without a track record of fulfilling them.

12.2.2 The Impact of Corruption and Scandals

Biden's political career has been marred by allegations of corruption and scandals. From his involvement in the Ukraine scandal to the questionable business dealings of his family members, the evidence uncovered by the House Committee has shed light on the extent of Biden's ethical shortcomings. This serves as a stark reminder of the importance of integrity and ethical conduct in public office. The American people deserve leaders who prioritize the interests of the nation over personal gain.

12.2.3 The Consequences of Undermining the United States

Perhaps one of the most significant lessons from Biden's betrayal is the consequences of undermining the United States. Through his foreign policy decisions and questionable alliances, Biden has weakened America's standing on the global stage. This has not only compromised national security but also eroded the trust and respect that other nations once had for the United States. It is a reminder that strong leadership and a clear vision for America's role in the world are crucial for maintaining our position as a global leader.

12.2.4 The Importance of Transparency and Accountability

Biden's presidency has been marked by a lack of transparency and accountability. From his refusal to address the concerns raised by the House Committee to his avoidance of tough questions from the media, Biden has demonstrated a disregard for the principles of open and honest governance. This serves as a reminder of the importance of holding our leaders accountable and demanding transparency in their actions. Without transparency and accountability, trust in our democratic institutions is eroded, and the foundations of our democracy are weakened.

12.2.5 The Need for Rebuilding America

The betrayal of Biden's political career has left America in a state of decline. From the border crises to the economic challenges of inflation, the consequences of his actions have been felt by the American people. As we reflect on these lessons, it becomes clear that rebuilding America is essential. We must prioritize policies that strengthen our economy, secure our borders, and restore faith in our democratic institutions. It is only through a collective effort to rebuild and restore that we can overcome the damage caused by Biden's betrayal.

In conclusion, the betrayal of Joseph Biden's political career has left a lasting impact on the United States. From false promises to corruption and scandals, his actions have undermined the trust of the American people and weakened our nation. As we reflect on these lessons, it is crucial that we learn from the mistakes of the past and work towards rebuilding America. By prioritizing transparency, accountability, and strong leadership, we can ensure a brighter future for our great nation.

12.3 Rebuilding America

As the United States grapples with the aftermath of Joseph Biden's political
career, it is crucial to reflect on the damage caused and consider the path
towards rebuilding the nation. The betrayal experienced under Biden's
leadership has left a lasting impact on various aspects of American society,
including the economy, national security, and public trust. However, amidst
the challenges, there is an opportunity to learn from the mistakes and work
towards a brighter future.

12.3.1 Restoring Economic Stability

One of the pressing issues that need to be addressed in rebuilding America is
the economic stability of the nation. Under Biden's presidency, inflation has
soared to alarming levels, causing significant hardships for American families.
To rebuild, it is essential to implement sound economic policies that prioritize
fiscal responsibility, reduce government spending, and promote job creation.
By fostering an environment conducive to business growth and innovation, the
nation can regain its economic strength and provide opportunities for its
citizens.

12.3.2 Strengthening National Security

Another critical aspect of rebuilding America is the restoration of national
security. Biden's foreign policy decisions have raised concerns about the
nation's standing on the global stage. It is imperative to reassess alliances and
relationships, ensuring that they align with America's national interests. By
prioritizing the security of the nation and its citizens, the United States can
regain its position as a global leader and protect its interests effectively.

12.3.3 Restoring Trust and Transparency

The betrayal experienced under Biden's leadership has eroded public trust in
the government. Rebuilding America requires a commitment to transparency
and accountability. It is essential to restore faith in the political system by

holding elected officials to the highest ethical standards and ensuring that they are held accountable for their actions. By fostering a culture of transparency and open dialogue, the nation can rebuild trust between the government and its citizens.

12.3.4 Addressing Immigration and Border Security

The border crises and immigration challenges that have plagued the nation under Biden's presidency cannot be ignored in the process of rebuilding America. It is crucial to develop comprehensive immigration policies that prioritize both humanitarian concerns and national security. By securing the borders and implementing fair and efficient immigration processes, the United States can regain control over its borders and restore order to the immigration system.

12.3.5 Investing in Education and Innovation

To rebuild America, it is essential to invest in education and innovation. By prioritizing quality education for all Americans, the nation can equip its citizens with the skills and knowledge necessary to thrive in a rapidly changing world. Additionally, fostering a culture of innovation and supporting research and development can drive economic growth and position the United States as a global leader in technology and innovation.

12.3.6 Healing Social and Cultural Divisions

The political climate under Biden's presidency has exacerbated social and cultural divisions within the nation. Rebuilding America requires a concerted effort to heal these divisions and foster unity. By promoting dialogue, understanding, and respect, the nation can bridge the gaps that have divided communities and work towards a shared vision for the future.

12.3.7 Restoring America's Standing on the Global Stage

Undermining the United States' standing on the global stage has been a consequence of Biden's foreign policy decisions. Rebuilding America necessitates a reevaluation of these decisions and a renewed commitment to protecting the nation's interests. By engaging in strategic diplomacy, fostering strong alliances, and advocating for American values, the United States can regain its position as a respected global leader.

12.3.8 Engaging the Media Responsibly

The media's role in shaping public perception cannot be overlooked in the process of rebuilding America. It is crucial to encourage responsible and unbiased reporting, holding the media accountable for their actions. By promoting a diverse range of perspectives and ensuring the dissemination of accurate information, the nation can foster an informed citizenry and strengthen its democratic foundations.

In conclusion, rebuilding America after the betrayal experienced under Joseph Biden's political career requires a multifaceted approach. It involves restoring economic stability, strengthening national security, rebuilding trust and transparency, addressing immigration and border security, investing in education and innovation, healing social and cultural divisions, restoring America's standing on the global stage, and engaging the media responsibly. By learning from the mistakes of the past and working towards a shared vision for the future, the United States can emerge stronger and more resilient than ever before.

12.4 Moving Forward

As the American people reflect on the political career of Joseph Biden, it becomes clear that his tenure has been marked by deception, corruption, and a disregard for the well-being of the nation. From his early years in the New Castle County Council to his time as Vice President and ultimately President, Biden's actions have had far-reaching consequences for the United States. Now, as we look to the future, it is crucial to learn from the mistakes of the past and chart a new course for our nation.

12.4.1 Restoring Integrity and Trust

Moving forward, it is imperative that we prioritize integrity and trust in our political leaders. The betrayal experienced under Biden's leadership has left a deep scar on the American psyche. To heal and rebuild, we must demand transparency, accountability, and ethical conduct from our elected officials. It is essential to elect leaders who prioritize the interests of the American people above personal gain and partisan agendas.

12.4.2 Strengthening the Economy

One of the most pressing challenges facing the United States is the state of our economy. The policies implemented by the Biden administration have contributed to skyrocketing inflation, job losses, and a decline in economic growth. To move forward, we must focus on implementing sound economic policies that promote job creation, reduce government spending, and encourage investment. By fostering a business-friendly environment and supporting small businesses, we can rebuild our economy and provide opportunities for all Americans.

12.4.3 Securing the Border

The border crisis that unfolded under Biden's watch has had severe implications for national security and humanitarian concerns. Moving forward, it is crucial to address this issue head-on. We must secure our borders, enforce immigration laws, and implement a fair and efficient immigration system. By prioritizing the safety and well-being of American citizens while also upholding our values as a nation of immigrants, we can find a balanced and sustainable approach to immigration.

12.4.4 Restoring America's Standing on the Global Stage

Biden's foreign policy decisions have undermined America's standing in the world. From the hasty withdrawal from Afghanistan to the strained relationships with key allies, our nation's reputation has suffered. Moving forward, we must prioritize rebuilding alliances, promoting democratic values, and advancing our national interests. By engaging in principled diplomacy and projecting strength, we can regain the respect and leadership that the United States deserves on the global stage.

12.4.5 Investing in Education and Innovation

To ensure a prosperous future, we must invest in education and innovation. By prioritizing quality education for all Americans, we can equip our workforce with the skills needed to thrive in a rapidly changing world. Additionally, fostering a culture of innovation and supporting research and development will drive technological advancements and economic growth. By investing in our people and embracing innovation, we can position the United States as a global leader in the 21st century.

12.4.6 Bridging Divisions and Restoring Unity

The political climate in America has become increasingly divisive and polarized. Moving forward, it is crucial to bridge these divisions and restore a sense of unity among the American people. We must prioritize civil discourse, respect differing viewpoints, and find common ground on the issues that affect us all. By fostering a culture of understanding and cooperation, we can heal the wounds of division and work towards a brighter future for our nation.

12.4.7 Empowering the American People

Ultimately, the power to shape the future of America lies in the hands of its citizens. Moving forward, it is crucial for the American people to remain engaged, informed, and active participants in the political process. By holding our elected officials accountable, participating in local and national elections, and advocating for the issues that matter to us, we can ensure that our voices are heard and that our democracy thrives.

In conclusion, the political career of Joseph Biden has been marred by betrayal, corruption, and a disregard for the well-being of the American people. As we look to the future, it is essential to learn from the mistakes of the past and chart a new course for our nation. By prioritizing integrity, strengthening the economy, securing the border, restoring America's standing on the global stage, investing in education and innovation, bridging divisions, and empowering the American people, we can rebuild and restore the greatness of the United States. The path ahead may be challenging, but with determination and a commitment to the principles that define us as a nation, we can create a brighter future for all Americans.

www.ingramcontent.com/pod-product-compliance
Lightning Source LLC
Chambersburg PA
CBHW050816260726
48660CB00004B/1461